Modern Tarot:

A practical guide to reading tarot in the 21st century

Latte Books | London

CONTENTS

INTRODUCTION

Learning how to use tarot cards for divination may seem like a daunting process. There is so much to memorize, various symbols, maintaining mindfulness of numerology and astrology, and many other aspects that can make the journey intimidating. However, it does not have to be a metaphysical odyssey.

Throughout this guide are explanations of symbols, themes (spirituality, health, love, money, travel, etc.), and even meditations associated with reversed cards to help you understand each of them as unique signposts on your tarot journey.

While this book is meant to help you explore the meanings and layers of each card, please treat them as general guidelines and not a finite resource. Take note of how your cards speak to you and how you manage to incorporate your authentic voice into your readings – whether for yourself or others.

Additionally, different tarot or oracle decks may have varied interpretations – even if their core message somewhat aligns with Rider-Waite-Smith tarot symbolism. Trust your intuition, but when things seem vague, unclear, or simply confusing, you may use this guide as a fellow traveler on the road through the tarot.

TAROT HISTORY & USE

A Brief History of Tarot

There are quite a few theories regarding the exact origins of the tarot. It is believed that tarot may have come from the Mamluk Empire (Modern Egypt), stemming from the rest of the Middle East and its passion for card games. It was believed that soldiers of this empire played with cards divided into four different suits (coins, batons, cups, and swords) and included court cards, like what we see in playing cards today. However, this fondness of card games is said to originate from China.

As Europeans adopted the card game practice, it evolved to include cultural symbolism and imagery that varied from the Islamic tradition, which didn't include the human form. However, the earliest form of what we know as a tarot deck is said to have emerged from Northern Italy in the early 15th century.

The Visconti-Sforza deck was commissioned as a luxury, hand-painted work of art for Francesco Sforza in 1441. It expanded upon the initial four-suit deck to include 22 *trionfi*, resulting in 78 cards. This is what we know today as the Major Arcana (Greater Mysteries) and the Minor Arcana (Lesser Mysteries). The commissioned artwork has been attributed to Bonifacio Bembo, who specialized in early-Renaissance murals and pieces that appealed to the Visconti-Sforza family and became known as *I Tarocchi dei Visconti*. Today, the Visconti-Sforza deck is the oldest known tarot deck in the world.

Fast forward to the latter half of the 15th century, French onlookers began adopting *I Tarocchi* and began calling it Tarot. While it appeared to start as a game, it didn't appear to be a clear divination tool until the 18th century in English and French social events. In the 19th century, societies

1

of occult enthusiasts began to emerge through sects such as Esoteric Freemasonry and Hermetic Order of the Golden Dawn.

In the 20th century, the Rider-Waite-Smith deck emerged and represents the classic deck we know today in the English-speaking world, thanks to the artistry of the innovative Pamela Colman Smith in 1909. In the French-speaking world, the Marseille deck tends to be the gold standard.

Here in the 21st century, we continue to use tarot to grow and learn about ourselves and the world around us, to connect to our Higher Self and Source. As the tarot communicates to us with the help of our intuition, a world of possibilities opens before us.

Connecting Through Tarot

Before diving into clearing space for a tarot reading or the meanings of various cards, it's essential to spend time connecting with a deck that is, in a sense, calling your name. You may be drawn to a particular deck due to its art or its unmistakable vibration, but it's important to take the time to both connect and be present when it comes to reading tarot.

Tarot is far more than a mere card game. It's a marvelous resource for tapping into your intuition, self-discovery, and assisting others on their personal journey to their Higher Self. When used mindfully, your connection with the Universe becomes more apparent, and the messages you seek are far more apparent. However, there can be positive and negative uses in the age of YouTube and online tarot readings. It's important to note that tarot should not be used for psychic spying (peering into another person's life without their consent), asking the same questions to get a preferred response, or using them to inflict negative energy upon others. Bear in mind that the energy vibration you put out toward others can also impact your overall vibration.

Tarot can bring about a tremendous shift in perspective if you allow it, and it's necessary to take your time choosing your preferred decks. For beginners, it may be helpful to start with the Rider-Waite-Smith deck to get comfortable with the symbolism and possibly keep a tarot journal to develop a relationship with your cards.

While the tarot is not a substitute for healthy human interaction, it can provide a boost in your vision of the world around you. Tarot can also help provide insight into improved situational and social awareness by allowing you to see a multidimensional perspective of life.

In the tarot journey, you could be provided meaningful messages on your own path to your Higher Self, and by raising your own vibration, you could potentially help light the way for others. What a gift!

In choosing your deck, it's imperative to acknowledge the power of your inner voice. Sometimes, you may gravitate toward a particular deck for an unknown reason. Perhaps the artwork isn't your usual preference, but something about it is pulling you to it. Trust that voice. Other times, you may acquire a new visually stunning deck, but nothing seems to be allowing you to connect to it properly. Trust that feeling, too. By trusting your own personal guidance in selecting a deck, you're opening yourself up for trusting your authentic voice on the tarot journey, which is essential.

Before Reading Tarot

Before you begin reading with your tarot deck, it's essential to get into a mindful state – a state of presence. What does that mean? It's removing distractions from your environment and getting into a mindset of being completely in tune with what you're doing. Regardless of whether you're reading for yourself or others, it's important to give your full and undivided attention. You deserve it, as well as anyone you choose to read for along the way. In short, respect your time and space – and that of other people.

Additionally, it may be helpful to you to spend time getting to know your cards and finding a "home" for them where you live. It's advisable to protect the energy of your cards with a cleansing method of your choice – sage, crystals, etc. – but to also place it in a part of your home where its energy can be respected and not exposed to other people's energy. You may choose a top drawer dedicated to neatly kept personal items or a box exclusively set aside from your metaphysical practices and magick.

No matter what you choose, think of a proper place where the tarot deck(s) can be safe, respected, and protected from the interference of external energies. Tarot is a lot like the relationships you keep – both with yourself and others. The work you put into your tarot journey may also be reflected in the way you treat yourself and others.

Next, we'll discuss clearing your space, reading for yourself, and reading for others before moving on to tarot symbolism.

Clearing Space

Clearing space and inviting positive energy into your environment before a tarot reading is easy to do and essential for a quality tarot reading. You can choose a specific area within your home where you like to read your tarot cards or set up for a tarot reading after clearing your dining room table. Regardless of your budget, you can set good intentions and elevate the environmental vibration by intentionally creating a space for your readings.

For example, you can start a cleared and clean desk space or a table. Next, you can lay a cloth used explicitly for tarot readings, apply your preferred crystals, and burn sage or palo santo to set the tone. Whichever methods call your name, trust in the power of your voice and respect your environment in the process.

After you've set up, you can practice a preferred form of meditation or ritual to get into a mindset of being fully present. Focus your energy onto your cards and invite spirit guides, angels, ancestors, or whichever entity you want to work within, aligning yourself with Source to receive messages. Once you've achieved a calm and receptive mindset, you can begin preparing your deck to read. Once again, you can use a specific ritual of your choice to clear your cards before and after your readings.

As soon as you're ready, set your intentions for the reading as clearly as possible. Focus on the answers you seek for clarity and express gratitude for this moment in time. As soon as you're ready, you can begin to shuffle. Before you start, you can also cut your deck three times to the left with your left hand.

Once you start shuffling, you might notice cards start jumping out of the deck. You can choose whether to accept those cards – especially if they're still facing down. Finally, another tidbit to keep in mind in your readings is reversals. You might notice some readers do not incorporate reversals, but it is recommended in this book that you should keep them in the reading to explore themes and messages as thoroughly as possible. Reversals come with their own lessons and meditations in this text to gain further insight into the messages and lessons you need to process to raise your vibration and accomplish your goals.

Reading for Yourself

You may benefit from connecting with your tarot by practicing with yourself first. Reading tarot is an art form and pulling a card a day as a habit and documenting your reactions and meditations on the symbolism in a tarot journal could be highly beneficial. Allow your intuition to lead you through your tarot journey, and you'll find that you'll begin to trust your inner voice more and more with practice.

When reading for yourself, clear your space, meditate, and set your intentions for the reading—express respect and gratitude for yourself, your surroundings, and the Universe. Enjoy your journey.

Reading for Others

As with reading for yourself, it's imperative to extend the same respect and gratitude for time, space, and people when reading for others. It's also essential to protect your own energy in the process through a preferred grounding technique and protective rituals of your choice.

Reading for others, especially when you're new to tarot, can be intimidating, but it can also be an exciting and rewarding process. No matter where you are on your journey, it's a great habit to be mindful of all energies around you and develop a sound self-awareness that will keep you mindful and present.

Regardless of the messages communicated through tarot and your intuition, it's important to be mindful of how you deliver such messages. Remember that the recipient can take readings as they resonate, and messages are not written in stone and are guides to what can happen if certain behaviors are implemented or changed. Everyone is different, so be vigilant in protecting your energy and space while keeping your intentions pure. With that said, regardless of who you're reading for, you must also be ready to compartmentalize your own feelings regarding the desired outcome. Energies of other people can be dynamic, draining, or overwhelming, so be sure to actively remain aware of those vibrations and respond to them accordingly.

In short, remain as objective and receptive to answers – no matter what they may be – as possible and protect your energy. Everyone has their own free will and how to respond, but you must also reinforce that your guidance is simply providing them with options, that everyone has their own choices to make. Source speaks in various ways, and while some messages may be confusing at first, it's helpful to stay as impartial as possible. If you have difficulty keeping yourself out of the reading, it's advisable to keep practicing until you can be objective.

SYMBOLISM

The visual aspect of the tarot brings tremendous insight if you allow it. If you're starting with a Rider-Waite-Smith deck – which is recommended for beginners in the learning process – you may notice themes and patterns in the imagery throughout the deck. From numerology to Kabbalistic or Egyptian symbols, the tarot is a treasure trove of mysteries and secrets. You don't have to know all these details intimately at first, but the background of each card may help in remembering what the cards mean and how you can best communicate its messages. It's also just as important to look for a recurring pattern of suits, numbers, or themes.

Some of the symbolism and extra layers to explore are listed as the following:

- **Major Arcana Planets** – If you're interested in implementing astrology in your readings, this could be helpful to know.
- **Major Arcana Zodiac Signs** – If you're looking to identify a key person the reading may be highlighting, these cards stand out more prominently.
- **Minor Arcana Zodiac Signs** – If you're looking for other people or those with strong placements, Minor Arcana cards can also point to specific people referenced in the message.
- **Numerology** – How numbers provide their messages and insights throughout the reading.

- **Court Cards** – How Pages, Knights, Queens, and Kings communicate and who they may indicate in a reading.
- **Rider-Waite-Smith Imagery** – Understand the symbols and secrets within the card and how they tell a story.

Major Arcana Planets

These Major Arcana cards have a planet and an element assigned. They are not limited to one astrological sign and can help sort through various energies.

0. The Fool: Uranus (Air)

I. The Magician: Mercury (Earth & Air)

II. The High Priestess: Moon (Water)

III. The Empress: Venus (Earth & Air)

X. The Wheel of Fortune: Jupiter (Fire)

XII. The Hanged Man: Neptune (Water)

XVI. The Tower: Mars (Fire)

XIX. The Sun: Sun (Fire)

XX. Judgement: Pluto (Water)

XXI. The World: Saturn (Earth)

Major Arcana Zodiac Signs

IV. The Emperor: Aries

V. The Hierophant: Taurus

VI. The Lovers: Gemini

VII. The Chariot: Cancer

VIII. Strength: Leo

IX. The Hermit: Virgo

XI. Justice: Libra

XIII. Death: Scorpio

XIV. Temperance: Sagittarius

XV. The Devil: Capricorn

XVII. The Star: Aquarius

XVIII: The Moon: Pisces

Minor Arcana Zodiac Signs

Aries
King of Wands
Two of Wands: 1st decan of Aries (March 21-30) Mars
Three of Wands: 2nd decan of Aries (March 31-April 10) Sun
Four of Wands: 3rd decan of Aries (April 11-20) Venus

Taurus
King of Pentacles
Knight of Pentacles
Five of Pentacles: 1st decan of Taurus (April 21-30) Mercury
Six of Pentacles: 2nd decan of Taurus (May 1-10) Moon
Seven of Pentacles: 3rd decan of Taurus (May 11-20) Saturn

Gemini
King of Swords
Eight of Swords: 1st decan of Gemini (May 21-31) Jupiter
Nine of Swords: 2nd decan of Gemini (June 1-10) Mars
Ten of Swords: 3rd decan of Gemini (June 11-20) Mercury

Cancer
King of Cups
Two of Cups: 1st decan of Cancer (June 21-30) Venus
Three of Cups: 2nd decan of Cancer (July 1-11) Mercury
Four of Cups: 3rd decan of Cancer (July 12-21) Moon

Leo
Queen of Wands
Knight of Wands
Five of Wands: 1st decan of Leo (July 22-August 1) Saturn
Six of Wands: 2nd decan of Leo (August 2-11) Jupiter
Seven of Wands: 3rd decan of Leo (August 12-22) Mars

Virgo
Queen of Pentacles
Eight of Pentacles: 1st decan of Virgo (August 23-September 1) Sun
Nine of Pentacles: 2nd decan of Virgo (September 2-11) Venus
Ten of Pentacles: 3rd decan of Virgo (September 12-22) Mercury

Libra
Queen of Swords
Two of Swords: 1st decan of Libra (September 23-October 2) Moon
Three of Swords: 2nd decan of Libra (October 3-12) Saturn
Four of Swords: 3rd decan of Libra (October 13-22) Jupiter

Scorpio
Queen of Cups
Knight of Cups
Five of Cups: 1st decan of Scorpio (October 23-November 1) Mars
Six of Cups: 2nd decan of Scorpio (November 2-12) Sun
Seven of Cups: 3rd decan of Scorpio (November 13-22) Venus

Sagittarius
Page of Wands
Eight of Wands: 1st decan of Sagittarius (November 23-December 2)
             Mercury
Nine of Wands: 2nd decan of Sagittarius (December 3-12) Moon
Ten of Wands: 3rd decan of Sagittarius (December 13-21) Saturn

Capricorn
Page of Pentacles
Two of Pentacles: 1st decan of Capricorn (December 22-30) Jupiter
Three of Pentacles: 2nd decan of Capricorn (December 31-Jan 9) Mars
Four of Pentacles: 3rd decan of Capricorn (January 10-19) Sun

Aquarius
Knight of Swords
Page of Swords
Five of Swords: 1st decan of Aquarius (January 20-29) Venus
Six of Swords: 2nd decan of Aquarius (January 30-February 8) Mercury
Seven of Swords: 3rd decan of Aquarius (February 9-18) Moon

Pisces
Page of Cups
Eight of Cups: 1st decan of Pisces (February 19-28) Saturn
Nine of Cups: 2nd decan of Pisces (March 1-10) Jupiter
Ten of Cups: 3rd decan of Pisces (March 11-20) Mars

Numerology

Numbers provide their own messages and insights throughout tarot readings. Numerology is the study of numbers that relate to human life. Numerologists use these numbers to understand personality, relationships, aptitude, and paths in life. Numerology has both an esoteric meaning and a known usage for everyday people.

The digits 1-9 are called the 'master numbers' because they're especially significant on a metaphysical level. Esoteric meanings include deeper spiritual understanding about separate lives, planes, or existences. Numeric symbology varies depending on which metaphysical school you subscribe to - modern numerologists often believe specific numbers have distinct vibrations associated with them.

Numerology is a metaphysical science that studies the meaning of numbers in our lives, their influence on us, and how they shape who we are and what opportunities come into our lives. Numeric vibrations also define an individual's path in life, with higher vibration numbers being better choices for career paths. In comparison, lower vibrational numbers indicate jobs that aren't suited to that person. With regards to tarot, we can explore the deeper spiritual meaning of numbers we see in the cards based on their esoteric qualities, also known as vibrational energies.

Zero: Zero signifies a blank slate, a new beginning, or the unknown. Zero is a symbol of possibilities and potential, as well as hope. The symbolism of this number is neutral - it does not have positive nor negative connotations. The zero is often used in Numerology to enhance other numbers by adding their vibrational energy or changing the subject's path. Zero can also be a placeholder when working with large numerological sums.

One or Ace: Aces or Ones signify a fresh start or new beginning. A change of location or a new attitude can completely alter the course of your life. This number is associated with leadership, self-reliance, ambition, and pioneering. Numeric vibrations of ones are powerful, and one is also associated with being a trailblazer and risk-taker that can pave the way for others. Ace cards indicate that you have unlimited potential that hasn't been tapped into yet. It can also represent the masculine energies of the Divine and is associated with the Root Chakra.

Two: Two is associated with duality, cooperation, and diplomacy. Its energy is about balance, harmony, partnership, and teamwork. It also represents love, affection, nurturing, and warmth. It may also indicate that you need to find the middle ground and balance between opposing forces, whether it is independence or having a partner. It is associated with forming close friendships and lasting relationships based on love and friendship, in addition to the power of intuition. It symbolizes the spectrum of Divine energies, both feminine and masculine, while also representing the Sacral Chakra.

Three: Three is associated with multiple roles, skills, and talents. Three indicates that you should focus on what you can do to improve and perfect your talents and skills. It is symbolic of growth, creativity, self-expression, and imagination. Numeric vibrations point to the importance of the cooperation of multiple entities toward creative endeavors and success. It is associated with the Solar Plexus Chakra.

Four: The numerological meaning of four includes stability, structure, security, loyalty, and family values. Four represents solid foundations built from strong traits such as hard work and responsibility. It encourages people to stick to their goals and principles no matter what anyone else says or does. It is associated with the Heart Chakra and represents standing one's ground - for better or worse.

Five: Numerological meanings of five are associated with change, travel, adventure, and unpredictability. Numeric vibrations related to the number five indicate that you should embrace your multiple facets - both good and bad. It indicates potential challenges, sudden changes, or life lessons designed to make you more resilient. Five represents the Throat Chakra and is associated with communication, accepting change when necessary, and finding new paths to freedom. Five also represents risk-taking which is an integral part of being successful.

Six: Numerology meanings of six are about partnership, labor, nurturing love, generosity, beauty, perfectionism, cooperation. Numeric code six encourages people to invest time in cultivating talents while embracing others' strengths as well. Numeric vibrations of the number six also symbolize hard work, social responsibility, and everyday responsibilities. It represents the Third Eye Chakra and is associated with channeling intuition.

Seven: Numerology meanings of seven are about creativity, magic, restlessness, curiosity, introspection. Seven encourages people to slow down and reflect on the world around them instead of rushing through life. Numeric vibrations of the number seven also symbolize finding your voice, which may not be the loudest but has merit, nonetheless. Numeric vibrations point to searching for an inner truth or strength that can only be found through deep reflection. It is associated with the Crown Chakra and is symbolic of seeking enlightenment and awareness of all things surrounding you, both seen and unseen.

Eight: Numerological meanings of number eight are about commitment, self-discipline, power, authority, and change brought by forces outside your control. Eight encourages you to find ways to accommodate change instead of struggling against it. Numeric vibrations point to the importance of giving others a chance since they are not static beings but are constantly evolving. Numeric vibrations also indicate that you should take time to recharge after facing too many challenges or obstacles at once. Eight is also associated with the Solar Plexus Chakra and symbolizes growth, productivity, independence, and power.

Nine: Numerology meanings of nine are about endings and completion. It indicates that you should focus on the things you have accomplished thus far in your journey as well as what is yet to come. Numerology vibrations of the number nine also indicate a time for review, reflection, and a sort of "cleansing" or "catharsis." It represents the Root Chakra which governs your sense of security and belonging in this world. Nine encourages people to find their inner strength when facing adversity, especially from forces beyond your control.

Ten: Numerology meanings of ten symbolize accomplishment and completion. Numeric vibrations point to a time for celebration since tasks have been completed and goals reached. Ten also represents karma and indicates that if you put positive energy out into the world, it will return to you. Numeric vibrations of the number ten represent both physical and spiritual happiness associated with transcendence. Numerological code ten is associated with the Sacral Chakra, which governs your emotions, sexuality, creativity, fertility, relationships, psychic abilities, intuition, trustworthiness, imagination.

Court Cards

Court Cards are usually depicted as people in the Minor Arcana and consist of Pages, Knights, Queens, and Kings. They can often communicate specific people and their personality traits in a reading.

Pages in tarot typically refer to a person who is youthful and has a lot of energy. They may also indicate that the one is currently learning something new or involved in their education. It can also indicate the arrival of new messages. The Page symbolizes the need to pay attention to what one is studying or people who carry the Page's traits, as this could become critical later.

Knights typically represent younger people or those with youthful energy who are traveling and doing well with their life path but may still need time to grow and evolve. The Knight often indicates that someone coming into your life will be very exciting because this person will provide motivation and inspiration to continue growing and exploring different options for themselves. It indicates travel and sudden changes.

Queens usually refer to someone with predominantly feminine energy. The Queen is independent, strong-willed, and often very nurturing as a leader. Queens represent people with strong feminine energy who are involved in their community or family, whether they are married with children or not. Queens can also indicate that one is working hard to see a goal or project through to fruition. Queens are skillful, resourceful, and carry a pearl of ancient wisdom that turns aspirations into reality through patience and persistence.

Kings usually refer to someone with predominantly masculine energy. Kings may represent people in authoritative roles who may be resourceful in putting plans into action. Kings can also indicate that one is currently working to achieve a specific goal requiring mastery of a skill.

Rider-Waite-Smith Imagery

Understanding the symbols and secrets within the cards and how they tell a story can be helpful to you on your tarot journey and give detailed insights and messages. Tarot cards are rich in symbolism, and tarot readers would do well to take the time to understand these symbols to provide detailed insights. Tarot decks where all the images are stylized according to the Rider-Waite-Smith system, which Pamela Colman Smith designed, are helpful to learn as a beginner before moving onto other decks with different designs because much of the symbolism gets lost or missed. The following definitions are based on the images you'll find in the Rider-Waite-Smith deck as well as other decks with varying imagery.

Air: Messages, spiritual inspiration, intellect

Angel: An angel is a spiritual being that serves as a messenger of Source. They are reassuring signs of comfort, guidance, protection, and peace. Archangels are powerful angels that carry Source's messages to humans. Seeing an archangel in a reading signals that guidance, blessings, and protection are nearby or within you.

Ankh: This is an Egyptian symbol meaning "eternal life." The ankh is a powerful symbol of union, freedom, and immortality. Seeing this symbol in your reading means you are supported by the blessings of life or that there is something for which to be thankful.

Anubis: The Egyptian god of the Underworld and a guide through the Tarot journey. This symbol signals a new cycle or a beginning in your journey. Anubis also represents elevated consciousness, communication, and intellect.

Arch: Seeing this symbol in your reading means there is a new cycle starting or an advancement of spirit.

Armor: Symbolic of protection, willingness to confront challenges, and a determination to fight for what is right. There is protective energy surrounding you, as well as the potential for magic.

Astrological signs: Astrology influences tarot by providing insight into what motivates people at different periods of life based on their astrological signs. When symbols from astrology appear in a tarot reading, they offer guidance about how best to approach specific issues through an understanding of these planetary influences, houses, and traits of the respective sign.

Aura: This is the spiritual energy field of light surrounding each of us. Most people have an aura of colors around them that reflect information about their physical and emotional well-being and can be seen by those who are gifted with this sight. Tarot readers see these colors as significant in a reading and use them as signs for guidance and healing.

Badger: This card shows up in your tarot reading when spirit is concerned with your health. Seeing a badger in tarot symbolizes spirit's need to be vigilant about your physical well-being.

Balance/Scales: Balancing scales represent equality, justice, fairness, and harmony; Tarot cards where you see balance scales reassure that everything will turn out fair and equitable. It also shows that not getting what we want is sometimes necessary (or even better) and gives us what we need instead.

Bat: This card means the senses are activated through personal magic. You can see this as activating your magic, becoming aware of spiritual gifts, or being on the lookout for messages that will appear in the spread or around you.

Bear: Seeing a bear in your tarot reading signifies strength and wisdom, especially regarding family matters.

Bee: A bee signifies hard work, the ability to network, and royalty.

Beige: The color beige is associated with neutrality, openness, and exposure. Seeing beige in tarot readings signifies the need to stay neutral or non-committal because you'll gain more insight by doing so.

Belt: Possible limitations or restrictions pertaining to time.

Bench: A bench signifies rest, relaxation, or downtime. Tarot readings where you see benches are telling you to slow down and take it easy so you can gain more insight about what's going on or how to proceed with things.

Bicycle: Tarot cards where you see bicycles show that the coming events are imminent and will happen very soon. It also indicates that something has just ended, and new beginnings are around the corner, so you should be prepared for both possibilities.

Bird: Bird symbolism is considered as symbols of air energy, intuition, messages, and magic because they fly high above the earth where their keen eyes can spot things below that others cannot see. When you see a bird in your Tarot reading, it means you should trust your intuition or seek answers through the guidance of spirit guides. Freedom, messages to be received, and clairvoyance are also indicated.

Black: The color black indicates the feminine aspects of the spirit and psyche. It also indicates passive energy, secrets, or unknown circumstances.

Blindfold: Blindfolds signify people or situations that appear to be closed, blocked, or hidden. There may also be a sense of denial or avoidance of accepting the truth. Blindfolds could also indicate taking your mind off the material world to focus on introspection.

Blue: Seeing this color in a reading signifies focusing your energy on being present. Blue signifies that nothing new or different requires immediate action, so concentrate on things as they already exist and don't bother trying to change them. It is also indicative of intuition and inner peace.

Boat: Boats indicate water energy (emotions, instincts, survival). They also signify messages will soon arrive or possible movement – whether literal or figurative – is imminent.

Bonfire: Tarot cards with bonfires in them typically show where energy has been unleashed, and it's burning through stagnant situations making way for new growth.

Book: Books represent knowledge and wisdom. Tarot cards where you see books symbolize information about your future, advice for how to proceed with things, or lessons learned from past experiences. The appearance of a book in your tarot reading means you need to research more about the matter at hand and seek information via books (either physical copies or e-books) that will provide helpful details.

Boots: Seeing boots indicates that something is present that's keeping you on your feet and looking out for yourself. Keep track of everything going on around you.

Bottle: Seeing this symbol in your tarot reading indicates that you need to look for answers within yourself because they're right beside or within you—as close as one thought away.

Bowl: Tarot cards where you see a bowl signifies nourishment, relaxation, or comfort. It may also mean nourishment is needed to relax for future events.

Box: Seeing a box mean things are waiting for you to open them before they can reveal themselves to you; opening up the doors to your fears by having the courage or taking some risks in life can release these hidden emotions.

Bride/Groom: A tarot card that shows a bride or groom signifies that opportunities for growth are present, but nothing's being done or said because the energy has not been activated yet to bring marital matters into the forefront. When this symbolism appears, it means energies must first be activated before any messages can be delivered.

Bridge/Archway/Tunnel: This card indicates change is coming on its own instead of having to initiate something yourself. Changing your way of thinking about things may be necessary.

Broom/Dustpan: An indication of needing to clean up your environment or start new things, so you should be prepared for both possibilities.

Brown: Brown indicates earth energies, humility, and determination. It also indicates the mundane and ordinary aspects of life.

Bull: Seeing this animal is symbolic of Taurus as well as vitality, strength, and power. It also indicates wealth, abundance, and luxury. Bull symbolism is activated so you can harness divine inspiration for growth, change, and progress. It also indicates financial and success through direct methods rather than being reliant on others. You should embrace an aggressive and productive mindset towards life instead of being passive or stagnant. Success through strong effort.

Butterfly: Butterflies represent transformation and cycles of life because their life cycle involves metamorphosis. Seeing butterflies in a tarot reading provides messages that there are lessons to learn from your current situation, which will lead you to be transformed and more connected to your Higher Self.

Caduceus: This is the staff associated with Hermes/Mercury, the god of communication, travelers, boundaries, diplomacy, tricksters, merchants, thieves, athletics, weights, and measures—basically anything requiring skill in measurement, negotiation, or mediation. It signifies an action in pursuit of goals, doing one's best to succeed, or even a kundalini awakening.

Castle: Symbolic of actualizing material goals, society, and security. On the other hand, seeing castles could also indicate being held back or not being allowed to progress forward.

Cat: This animal represents transformation in many cultures and some readers interpret seeing a cat as an indication of readiness for change or that transformation is about to occur. A cat could also signal that you're allowing stress and anxiety to distract you, which can lead you down the wrong path. Seeing this symbol means you must relax and not let stress overtake your best interests. Cats also indicate the astral world, psychic powers, jumping timelines, and dark knowledge. It may also mean that there is too much negative energy around for positive progress right now, and to focus on cleansing your aura and environment.

Cauldron: A cauldron indicates opportunities and ideas that will bring changes in life, such as changing jobs or moving. It also means you should try new things and make bold choices because this is a time to shine and show off the skills learned through experience and trial and error.

Cave: Tarot cards with caves in them typically mean something of value has been discovered or uncovered. These discoveries are usually related to the subconscious (or dreaming) mind and often lead you to figuring out complicated issues or problems.

Chains: Tarot cards with chains in them typically show you may be feeling "chained" to circumstances, feelings, emotions, or situations. However, chains that are acknowledged can be broken through action or effort towards transformation for the better. Chains are often a symbol of self-imposed restrictions.

Chalice: Tarot cards with chalices in them typically mean you are seeking the truth; there is an emotional reason for this, and it is a need for inner healing. It symbolizes peace and harmony are within. It also represents a person who is calm, centered, and at peace who can create an environment of serenity and calm for everyone else as well.

Chair/Throne: Details on what a chair or throne represents vary between tarot card decks, but they may be seen as symbols for authority, power, control, confidence, success—the list goes on depending on the individual deck used. Seeing a throne or chair in your tarot reading means you have gained powerful skills that can help you achieve your goals.

Child: Seeing a child depicted in tarot indicates optimism and that you should be open to new opportunities. It may also mean needing to trust in Divine timing without any doubt or risk losing an important opportunity.

Circle: Process of completion, infinite cycles, or reaching a goal. This symbol means you must take some time to stop and think before making any choices you might want you to make.

City/Town: A tarot card with a city or town in it means you may be trying too hard. You may be trying to do everything yourself rather than trusting others or letting go of control when you should. It might also mean there are too many distractions holding you back from what cards want you to focus on right now.

Cloud: Seeing clouds indicates thought processes and the collective mind. Pay close attention to nearby cards as messages may be unclear, misleading, or confusing.

Clover: A Tarot card with a four-leaf clover in it indicates that opportunities will be coming your way. It also means that things are not as they appear—there are deeper meanings within the subconscious mind or the subconscious mind of someone else that needs to be revealed through intuitive development.

Construction Site: Seeing construction sites in your tarot reading usually mean that there is upheaval and change ahead.

Coffin: The coffin represents death or endings (as does seeing any coffin-shaped objects). Seeing coffins in tarot cards indicate the necessity of change. It may also indicate feelings of loss, sadness, or depression. Symbols of a coffin in your readings typically indicate an ending or closing of sorts, but it can also represent something ending so it can be replaced with something better. It may also indicate the death of ego or going through a life-changing emotional or spiritual transformation.

Crayfish: The crayfish represents feeling overwhelmed or stressed. It also indicates the unconscious mind or the early stages of a transformative experience.

Crescent Moon: Seeing a crescent moon indicates that readers should follow their intuition right now because it is coming from the heart. More specifically, many people see the crescent moon as being linked with goddess energy which can indicate Divine Feminine power.

Cross: Seeing a cross indicates the link between the spiritual and physical world. You may experience being "called" or "tested". Seeing crossed swords in tarot readings can represent not being able to move forward because of self-imposed limitations.

Crossroads: The symbolism behind crossroads is coming to an important, life-changing decision.

Crown: A crown typically represents authority, order, or dominance. It may also indicate being at the crossroads of consciousness and spiritual awakening. Seeing a crown means that if you have already achieved what you wanted through hard work, then you will receive additional rewards for your efforts. It may also mean that an ending is near and it's time for new beginnings.

Cube: An indicator of the physical, 3D world.

Cup: Water sign (Cancer, Scorpio, Pisces) energy. Cups also symbolize emotion, love, and relationships.

Dagger: In many tarot readings, seeing a dagger indicates feelings about yourself you should work through before making any decisions according to your intuitive impulses from your subconscious mind.

Dancer: Seeing a dancer in tarot is typically considered to be very positive because it indicates hope, moving forward, and new opportunities. Dancers are also associated with the element of air, which is connected to ideas, thoughts, communication, speeches, and writing.

Deer/Stag: A deer or stag typically means that an aspect of life needs attention in order for things to come together. Depending on how well you understand yourself, and your own power to overcome obstacles through strength of will, this journey will be as easy or as difficult as you make it.

Desert: The release of the material to focus on the journey within. It is symbolic of fire energy that is intense and possibly detached.

Devil: The ego, vices, and self-imposed enslavement to the material world.

Dog: A symbol of loyalty and having a protective energy around you.

Door: A portal or entranceway into another realm, dimension, or life chapter.

Dove: Symbolic of purity, peace, love, and guidance from Source.

Dragon: Indicative of power, authority, and vitality.

Eagle: Aspirations of the Higher Self. Scorpio at its highest evolved form as well as air signs. Also, see Phoenix.

Egg: Potential, ideas that are on the verge of manifesting into reality.

Ether: Indicates the fifth element and the spiritual dimension.

Eye: A symbol for spiritual vision, clairvoyance, and seeing beyond this realm.

Feather: Symbolic of air signs, but also Scorpio and eagle symbolism. It also represents communication, flight, and spiritual awakenings.

Fence: Indicates limitations or restrictions.

Field: Harvesting and reaping benefits of hard work.

Fish: The unconscious mind, emotions, hidden messages, ideas, and increases in abundance.

Flag: A message of arrival of messages of gifts of the spiritual world.

Flames/Fire: Fire sign (Aries, Leo, Sagittarius) energy that pertains to passion, creativity, and transformation.

Flowers: Symbolic of beauty, the reproductive system, and gratitude. It also represents the fruits of a creative endeavor manifesting.

Fruits & Vegetables: Reaping the benefits of hard work.

Garden: Solar plexus, subconscious mind, creativity, self-confidence, and abundance.

Globe: The collective, knowledge, and transcendence.

Grapes: Abundance, luxury, fertility, and ambition.

Green: Green symbolizes desire, healing, and abundance.

Grey: Symbolic of harmony, balance, or possible indecision.

Halo: Auric egg, pure consciousness, and the path to the Higher Self.

Hammer: Symbolic of physical labor and working hard toward achieving a goal.

Hand: Masculine and feminine energies. Giving and receiving spiritual insights as well as important messages.

Heart: Physical and spiritual union, emotion, relationships, and divine connection.

Hermit: Symbolizes the path to the Higher Self, taking a journey within and finding enlightenment.

Horse: Symbolic of vitality, progress, sensuality, and actual movement.

Ice: Ice indicates the status quo, fixed ideas, or stagnant thinking. A period of waiting and introspection is also indicated with ice.

Infinity: Symbolic of eternity, the cycle of life, and unity of all that exist in our Universe.

Iris: Love, healing, courage, messages, and new inspiration are indicated.

Jewels: Wisdom, love, and luxury.

Key: Unlocking mysteries or esoteric knowledge. When the keys are gold, they represent the conscious mind. When they are silver, they represent the subconscious mind.

Lamp: Heart chakra energy activation.

Lantern: The quest for truth and the Higher Self. Enlightenment and clarity will manifest.

Laurel: Victory.

Lead: Saturn energy. Karmic ties, time, responsibilities.

Leaves: Growth and vigor are indicated through personal development.

Lightning: Truth coming to light, sudden inspiration, reality checks are indicated with lightning. Possibilities of creative or destructive forces are at play.

Lilies: Innocence, fertility, and Divine Feminine power.

Lion: Symbolic of royalty, authority, and power. Also indicates sensual desires, Leo energy, pride, and courage.

Lotuses: These flowers typically represent new beginnings and happiness. They can also be representative of peace or positive feelings about something new coming into your life. Lotuses represent the crown chakra.

Mirror: Reflection, judgement, or facing the truth.

Moon: Divine Feminine energy. Secrets, hidden knowledge, the subconscious, and introspection.

Mountain: Represents challenges and obstacles to be overcome and severity can be indicated by the elevation seen in the card.

Nudity: Innocence and breaking free of dogmatic and patriarchal thinking. Being receptive to the messages of Source.

Ocean: Emotions, love, and the subconscious mind.

Oil: Prana, life force, or pure love.

Olive Branch: Peace, union, or conflict resolution.

Orange: Fire energy, extroversion, eccentric, and sensuality.

Owl: Magician energy, and wisdom.

Palm: Victory is at hand.

Path: The journey to the Higher Self.

Pentacle: Earth sign (Virgo, Capricorn, Taurus) energy. It also indicates the material world, wealth, and abundance.

Phoenix: Highest evolution of Scorpio. It also symbolizes dramatic transformation or rebirth.

Pillar: Seeking balance between spiritual and material world matters.

Pink: Feminine energy, thoughtfulness, youth, and romance are symbolic of the color pink.

Pomegranate: Fertility, cycle of life, transformation, and the underworld.

Pool: Womb energy, feminine energy, Moon energy.

Purple: Intuition, royalty, and renewal are symbolic of purple.

Pyramid: Symbolic of genius, ascension, and personal breakthroughs.

Rabbit: Earth energy – especially pertaining to Virgo – as well as fertility, connections with loved ones, and situational awareness.

Rainbow: Symbolic of Divine Feminine energy and peace.

Ram: Associated with Aries and Mars energy. Symbolic of courage under fire, action, impulsivity, and perseverance. Also seen in the Emperor card, which represents Aries.

Red: Red indicated passion, danger, fire energy, and vitriol.

Reptiles: Fire sign (Aries, Leo, Sagittarius) energy. It also represents kundalini activation and sensuality as it relates to primal instincts.

River: Life force, fluctuation of emotions, and rejuvenation.

Rod: Mastery, expertise, and rigorous discipline.

Rose: Red roses symbolize hope, passion, and Divine Masculine presence while white roses symbolize transformation and virtue.

Salamander: A nocturnal reptile that represents fertility, contemplation, and adaptability. Also, see Reptiles.

Scale: Balance, justice, truth, and Libra energy.

Scroll: Hidden knowledge and spiritual protection.

Snail: Self-sufficiency.

Snake: Symbolic of consciousness, wisdom, transformation, healing and sexuality.

Snow: Difficulties, trials, and rebirth.

Sphere: Cycles, creative progress, and earth energies.

Sphinx: Ancient wisdom, occult practices, and esoteric knowledge.

Spiral: Kundalini awakening and the elevation of consciousness.

Staff: Power, authority, and support.

Stained Glass: Seeing the macro picture of an issue or problem.

Star: Spiritual awakening and Aquarius energy. Wishes coming true and manifestation of spiritual gifts.

Sun: Divine Masculine energy, ego, creativity, and vitality.

Sunflower: Joy, optimism, and strength.

Swan: Elegance, activation of the manifestation process, and royalty.

Sword: Air sign (Aquarius, Gemini, Libra) energy. It symbolizes intellect, messages, and knowledge.

Throne: Authority and having support in endeavors.

Tomb: Transformations, rebirth, and the cycle of life and death to make way for new beginnings.

Tower: Impermanence of the material world, 3D thinking, conscious mind attempting to connect with the spiritual realm.

Town: Teamwork, security, and society.

Triangle: Pointing up (masculine energy), pointing down (feminine energy).

Trumpet: Awakening, sounds, and messages.

Veil: Hidden mysteries, blocked third eye, and delusional thinking.

Venus: Associated with Venus and Divine Feminine energies.

Wall: Material limitations, security, denial.

Wand: Fire sign (Aries, Leo, Sagittarius) energy. It symbolizes action, vitality, passion, and magic.

Water: Water sign (Cancer, Scorpio, Pisces) energy. It symbolizes emotions, relationships, and nurturing.

Wheat: Fertility, abundance, and symbolic of Virgo energy.

White: Conscious mind and what is made known, a physical or spiritual cleansing.

Wing: Freedom from the material world, flight, and communication.

Wolf: Conscious mind fueled by intense, and possibly destructive, desire. Untamed desires, parts of the subconscious mind that might be frightening.

Yellow: Sun energy, abundance, joy, creativity.

Yod: 10th letter of the Hebrew alphabet indicating Source is all around. It represents the method by which the blessing descends from the Divine through concentrated forms. Blessings are about to manifest as Yod flows down to the material world from Source.

MAJOR ARCANA

The Major Arcana is comprised of 22 cards that signify major life events, lessons, and messages. In tarot readings, the Major Arcana cards take precedence over all other card types. Tarot readers use these cards in a variety of different layouts or spreads. When people seek readings about their love life and important decisions in their present circumstances, they rely upon the Major Arcana to show them what lies in store for them in future situations that will play a significant role in their lives. Ultimately, the Major Arcana cards represent things that have a major effect on a person's life and circumstances.

0. The Fool

Overview: When the Fool appears, it indicates a sense of playfulness, adaptability, and childlike wonder. The Fool is ruled by Uranus and is not merely naïve, but can also be a trickster, manifesting possibilities under the guise of innocence. Remain adaptable in all that you aspire to do. The Fool is a paradox, meaning that you can wander into a situation where you are seemingly unaware of potential dangers, but have the confidence that you can manifest what you need. This card represents standing at a crossroads, but also indicates the importance of maintaining a sense of humor and childlike wonder. Your ability to adjust under stress is imperative at this time.

Love: This is a time to have fun and not take dating or relationships too seriously. However, don't let your playful attitude keep you from recognizing a quality long-term relationship. Keep things light and airy, but also pay attention to the signals that others send your way. Complacency kills romance.

Mind & Spirit: Wisdom and madness are indicated here. Trusting in the Universe that things will work out in its own time. You have more power and control over your life than you think. There is hidden wisdom in places you least expect.

Body: Be flexible and make time for self-care. Laughter may be the best medicine to de-stress and decompress after dealing with stressful events. Be wary of minor accidents.

Money: The need for balance between work and play. Cooperative efforts are best at this time when it comes to work and investments. A new job, position, or opportunity to earn more is on the horizon. A sudden stroke of good luck with money.

Travel: A new journey is about to begin! However, be mindful of where you are going. It is important to have fun along the way, but do not be careless either. Unforeseen circumstances may arise for the better.

Geography: Southern Europe, South America

Locations: Mountains, hiking locations, national parks, places where children play or learn, parties

0. The Fool Reversed

Overview: There may be tension and rigidity with those who surround you. This is a subtle nudge to keep your wits around you while you enjoy a new journey, project, or relationship. Try to trust in your instincts instead of hesitating. A new beginning is on the horizon and will happen regardless of whether you prepare.

Love: You may be experiencing more folly than wisdom in your love life. You might want more independence than you realize and are alienating potential partners or a current relationship in the process. Are you fearful of commitment? Or is it real intimacy that frightens you? When you take the leap of faith by opening up, you also allow space for great love to present itself.

Mind & Spirit: You may be feeling ambivalent about your current beliefs or traditions rooted in dogma. This may be the time to explore other belief systems that are more in line with your spiritual journey. Take the time to meditate and contemplate on what the ideal spiritual lifestyle consists of and be fearless in your pursuit.

Body: Be wary of accidents that stem from not being grounded in the present. Additionally, if you are experiencing health conditions with ambiguous diagnoses, be sure to get a second opinion or explore alternative means of healing. Don't neglect your physical or mental health at this time.

Money: Are you taking work or money a bit too seriously? You might be experiencing a bit of hesitation in taking risks financially or professionally. Trust in the Universe and things will work out. If you are thinking about a new job, now may be a good time to plan for a fresh new start. However, be extra careful in investments and purchases as you may overlook key numbers or details.

Meditations: Are you making a mountain out of a molehill? Is there an area of your life that would benefit from more flexibility? It's time to gain new perspective on your situation. Be open to learning something new, even if it may make you uncomfortable.

I. The Magician

Overview: The Magician is the card of manifestation, shapeshifting, and cloaking oneself in an invisible shroud of protection. This auspicious card is one that indicates movement across mystical boundaries and doorways into other dimensions. Pay attention to things that are unsaid as well as what is said, paying close attention to both verbal and nonverbal cues. It is indicative of trusting in the vibrations around you and those of whom you deal with. The Magician is ruled by Mercury and indicates that if you want something to happen, you have everything you need right now to manifest your goals.

Love: Manifesting a new relationship is possible now, and that power is in your hands. Your ideal partnership is not going to magically appear out of thin air – you're going to have to put yourself out there and work that magic. If you're already in an established relationship, there will be an increase in romantic magic through deepening intimacy and trying new things together. This card also indicates a need to get a better perspective on your love life and to manifest your ideal circumstances.

Mind & Spirit: You will possess the ability to conceal yourself, protecting yourself from harm and enemies. This is the time to master the art of camouflage as well as manifesting your dreams into reality. Trust in the spiritual undercurrents around you. If you need to try something new, this is the time to do so, but keep it to yourself. This also indicates a possible encounter with a spiritual/wellness mentor.

Body: Knowledge is power when it comes to health and wellness when the Magician appears. The Magician also emphasizes trusting one's sense of smell and hearing when possible. An improvement in health is on the horizon. If you are researching health and treatment options, expand your horizons by looking into different therapies and self-care activities to feel your best.

Money: Keeping your efforts discreet will enhance your ability to achieve success in work and finances. In terms of work, this indicates a possible promotion or new opportunities – but you must do the work and make it happen. Financial luck is indicated at this time and may appear from an unexpected source.

Travel: You are about to embark on an adventure that is both magically and spiritually life changing.

Geography: Africa

Locations: Live entertainment venues, laboratory, restaurant, library, expert offices, scientific foundations, or research organizations.

I. The Magician Reversed

Overview: The Magician in reverse is a call to go within to reassess any doubts about your personal power. Are you overlooking all the signs around you and dismissing synchronicities the Universe sends your way? The Magician reversed indicates you might not be present and grounded in ways that might hinder your progress.

Love: Are you afraid of your own inner magic? You might be overlooking important details in your relationships or losing faith in finding the right person. This may also mean you are wrestling with trusting in your authentic voice and setting healthy boundaries with others. You make your destiny – don't wait for it to happen for you. Courageously communicate your wants and needs or you will go unfulfilled.

Mind & Spirit: Now is the time to seek advice from an unconventional source and shop around for different means of seeking fulfillment. Try to talk with others and gain new perspectives. Now is the time to listen and process.

Body: Your overall health is predicted to improve, but seek the appropriate medical providers as needed. Give yourself time to heal and look for ways that you can practice self-care.

Money: It's time to shed the dead skin of the past if you want to see improvement in finances and professional goals. You might feel as though you're in a financial rut or displeased with your professional path. Now is the time to decide what's important for you to feel financially secure or professionally fulfilled.

Meditations: Be careful not to speak of your plans aloud to others. Your magic loses its power when you reveal your secrets. Do not let others know your plans until after they are achieved. You can best harness your magic when you honestly believe in yourself. Potential means absolutely nothing without intentional action.

II. The High Priestess

Overview: The High Priestess is an enchanting card brimming with mysticism, interweaving illusions, and Divine Feminine magic. It is ruled by the Moon. This card heralds an awakening of inner magic and creativity. You need to find a balance between work and play, physical and spiritual, and being aware of your inner power as much as your surroundings. Being assertive in your creativity is key. Don't solely rely on what your eyes see, trust your intuition as well. Your muse is speaking to you, and if you trust in your own inner moon magic, you can weave your dreams into reality. The number 8 is also a signpost.

Love: Don't beat around the bush in communicating matters of the heart. Be direct and clear regarding your intentions. Your physical attractiveness is heightened with the appearance of the High Priestess, but it also may indicate encountering an attractive person with strong feminine energy who is unavailable. Don't take advantage of others or violate anyone's boundaries.

Mind & Spirit: This is the time to express your spirituality or mental health wellness through creative outlets. Pay attention to the power of your dreams by writing them down, drawing out colors and symbolism, or whichever way you prefer to document them.

Body: If you're looking for answers regarding your health, you're likely to get some resolution soon but you have to be proactive about it. Be extra mindful of your diet, supplements, and exercise routines.

Money: Creative opportunities to improve finances through inventions, new invitations to innovative projects, or making systems more efficient. However, if you sense that any investment or financial opportunities seem too good to be true, then you're probably right. You have every right to ask questions if you feel uncomfortable about moving forward. Avoid all workplace drama when and where possible.

Travel: You may be intrigued by new languages and countries you've never visited. Something is nudging at you to learn more.

Geography: Argentina, Africa

Locations: An undisclosed location, speakeasy, library, study hall, secret meeting spots, psychic reader location, spiritual places.

II. The High Priestess Reversed

Overview: The High Priestess in reverse indicates a time to exercise patience. Do not waste energy in pushing for results. Intuition and awareness of one's own beauty are hindered. Lift the veil – the answers are right in front of you.

Love: It may be time to love yourself a bit more as you may be undervaluing yourself. Don't make any assumptions in love, speak up and clarify any lingering confusion. Not everyone speaks the same love language.

Mind & Spirit: This is a time for needed introspection and focus. Take back your power and trust your intuition to guide you. Write down your thoughts and listen to your inner voice. Are you noticing synchronicities or dream symbols that stand out? Seek guidance or, at minimum, write them down. Messages will become clearer later.

Body: Mind and body wellness is highlighted here and now might be the time to try a new class or wellness ritual. If you're dealing with an illness, seek a specialist or a second opinion. If something feels off about your health and you're not getting answers, advocate for yourself.

Money: Are you focusing on what others have instead of your own progress? This is a sign to pull back and evaluate what you really need in terms of financial stability or professional goals. Be careful of who you trust with money as someone is possibly being deceptive. If something is nudging your intuition, no matter how insignificant it may seem, trust that warning. Avoid large purchases or major investments at this time.

Meditations: Are you hesitant in listening to your inner voice? Are you avoiding addressing uncomfortable topics with those you care about? Now is the time to use creativity to destress and problem solve.

III. The Empress

Overview: The Empress is ruled by Venus and represents Divine Feminine energy at its most creative, fertile, and powerful. Her sexual prowess and intuition make for a wonderful omen when she appears in a reading. She is a leader who has a strong sense of justice and a powerful voice to communicate how she truly feels. She insists the use of language (verbal and body) to get her point across. Now is the time to use sound, vibration, and/or song to communicate. Trust in your creative energies. Your words carry power and intensity – use them wisely to manifest your goals. People are also quite drawn to you – romantically and/or platonically – at this time.

Love: You will experience more sensuality, intimacy, and passion. Your attractiveness also seems to be elevated with incoming attention and admiration from others. This is also a very fertile period – physically and psychologically. Long-term relationships begin or deepen in established relationships. If you're looking to have children or adopt, this is an auspicious time.

Mind & Spirit: You might find that chanting, binaural beats, or soothing music to be beneficial at this time. It is important to incorporate music into manifesting your dreams. People may seek you out for your wisdom and you are encouraged to share your knowledge with those who seek it. Heightened intuition is indicated so make time to meditate and reflect on your messages and visions. Unexpected altruism toward you is also indicated and the possibility of a wonderful adviser/mentor figure appearing in your life. The Universe is conspiring to help you succeed. Relax, and think positive thoughts! The birth of new ideas is afoot.

Body: If you or your partner are trying to have children, this is a wonderful sign. If this is not part of your life plan, exercise caution. You may also hear about someone close to you becoming pregnant. For general health, this is a suggestion to explore aromatherapy, acupuncture, or other alternative healing modalities.

Money: Financial luck in indicated especially concerning creative endeavors. An improvement in work and professional life or long-term stability. This is the time to put your creative ideas to work for you. Luck in money will persist, but also be sure to pay it forward by helping others in need. Maintain firm boundaries where needed but remember it's better to build a longer table to share, than a higher wall to keep others out.

Luxury, comfort of good food and friends, and healthy boundaries reverberate through this card. This is big queen energy, and with that said, you should also be highly assertive in getting what you want, too.

Travel: Taking a trip connected to wellness, recovery, or self-care is highly encouraged.

Geography: Europe, Southwest Asia

Locations: Home, maternity ward, mother's home, fertility clinic, hair or nail salons, high-end restaurants, orchards, and specialty shops.

III. The Empress Reversed

Overview: The Empress in reverse indicates a lack of relaxation in your life and/or blocks to your creativity. Everyone has the spectrum of Divine Feminine and Masculine within and this indicates an imbalance of energies. You may be wasting your energy in noncreative outlets and blocking your own progress as a result. Words and thoughts are power, so be careful of succumbing to negative self-fulfilling prophecies. Don't do the same thing over and over and expect a different result. Sometimes the rut you're in can also be a comfort zone.

Love: Trust your intuition in dating or long-term relationships. If you're single, you might find having to decide between potential love interests. You might be underestimating your attractiveness. This is also a possible indicator for a need for a self-esteem boost. Love yourself first before expecting someone else to love you.

Mind & Spirit: It's time to get centered and decompress through breathing exercises, meditation, or anything else that is designed to align mind, body, and spirit. Pay attention to subtle cues and when people slip information unintended before you. Seek the wisdom of a wise woman for guidance or inspiration.

Body: It's time to get outside and get some fresh air! If you're feeling stuck or stifled, a change of scenery involving some outdoor experience may be your much-needed medicine.

Money: When it comes to your work, you might wonder if you're getting proper credit or appreciation. This is possibly a misconception as your efforts are noticed. Build upon your communication if there is a work or financial misunderstanding. Visualize abundance and then plan accordingly.

Meditations: Are you practicing positive self-talk? Write down affirmations for your goals from relationships to prosperity. Your inner voice is powerful, so make sure it's saying the right things to help make way for a brighter future.

IV. The Emperor

Overview: Clear vision, authoritative power, and healing are indicated in this Divine Masculine archetype. This is a card that indicates drawing upon your visions – whether past or future – and putting theory into action. New perspectives on health, projects, and ambitions are unfolding. Conserve your energies to seize the right opportunities for you and seek a sense of inner balance throughout your journey. Be ready to make firm, objective decisions that lean toward logic and reason rather than intuition alone. Before you can fly, you also require a solid foundation. Expect news pertaining to the numbers 8 or 10 and manifestations arriving in 3s.

Love: Stability is key when the Emperor appears. To build a solid relationship, one must have healthy communication, boundaries, and a shared vision for the future. This card could also indicate a masculine figure emerging in your life who will provide insight (directly or indirectly) into your love life. You may be starting a relationship – or currently involved – with someone older than you or seems older in personality.

Mind & Spirit: Getting in touch with your inner voice and understanding visions from childhood are indicated here. Be assertive in communicating your needs and using your best judgment in making important decisions. Now is the time to seek structure and not getting lost in emotions but maintain a balance within to achieve your goals.

Body: Be mindful of health issues pertaining to eyes and sight. If you're experiencing vision changes, be sure to see your doctor. This is a time to be mindful of how your health choices impact aging. Holistic healing could be explored for additional health benefits, or you may consider taking on a healing profession. Pay attention to your vitals at your medical checkups or health monitors. This is also a great time to form a new exercise routine and/or diet.

Money: In work matters, be direct and follow through on your projects. Be aware of how you and your work is perceived and make decisions that are guided by logic rather than emotion. If you're looking for a new job, use the same rationale. Think about your own value proposition before embarking upon anything new. Now is the time to exercise caution and discipline in your finances and avoiding unnecessary spending. You can plan for a brighter future by making sound, mature decisions now.

Travel: A journey related to accomplishing professional or financial goals is indicated with the Emperor. Take charge of your destiny and move ahead with your plans using decisive strategy and the appropriate tactics for the situation.

Geography: East Asia, Europe, Argentina

Locations: Headquarters, royal palaces, government leader offices, CEO office, luxury hotel, or military bases.

IV. The Emperor Reversed

Overview: Knowing when to speak and controlling your words is indicated when the Emperor is in reverse. Someone may be hurt – you or someone you know – as a result of uncontrolled speech or arguments. Impatience, opportunism, and misguided energies are suggested and now may be the time to get grounded in your life. Energy expended on pointless drama or projects may end up costing your health eventually, so be mindful of where you invest your time. This is a big sign to exercise being present in all that you do. Someone older than you may be causing you frustration but take any advice that resonates with reason and discard the rest.

Love: You might be in a relationship or dating someone who is unorganized or chaotic. If you can't figure out how to make things work, move on quickly or else. Your love life needs a sense of order, and those who don't align with your life path may need to go on their way to other horizons.

Mind & Spirit: Pay attention to spiritual mentors coming into your life. Be aware of anyone who has questionable intentions and take your time in finding someone that connects with your path. Don't discount your own intuition. This is a time for developing your inner voice.

Body: Pay attention to health issues pertaining to the eyes as well as regular fitness and diet regimens. You may need a boost of self-discipline if your habits have fallen to the wayside. Seek medical assistance or fitness coaching as needed.

Money: You may benefit from financial guidance at this time to build structure for the future. It is ill-advised to ignore the need for budgeting and reigning in any superfluous spending. When it comes to work, tough decisions may be made and you might not appreciate the outcome and how it affects your workflow.

Meditations: Are you not following through on your commitments? Now is the time to exercise self-discipline and avoid taking on too much too soon.

V. The Hierophant

Overview: When the Hierophant appears, it may be time to change the old traditions to make way for new opportunities to manifest. It's a card that's rooted in dogma, tradition, and grounding oneself but it also suggests that you have the answers within you now and to trust your inner voice. Be mindful how religion factors into your life in addition to routines, rigid rules, patriarchal systems, and so on.

Love: This card signifies a push for a traditional relationship or being in a relationship where there is a clash of personality. Try to be diplomatic in problem-solving and general communication.

Mind & Spirit: Self-care rituals are suggested and to have a positive, healthy structure in your life. Set up and follow through on spiritual rituals that fit your journey. Make time in your schedule to regularly meditate and reflect.

Body: If you're experiencing health issues, refrain from sticking to solely alternative therapies and listen to your doctor. Improve your discipline in eating habits and exercise.

Money: You or someone you know may be seen as a professional leader or mentor. Finances and professional endeavors go well so long as you play by the rules. Seek financial guidance from a well-established institution or organization with a good reputation and avoid any trends or risks with investments. Focus on conserving your assets.

Travel: Upcoming travels may be heavy with traditional religious symbolism. Whether it's missions on California's coast or seeing an abundance of religious buildings, travel may involve dealing with authoritative, dogmatic figures, so be advised on avoiding confrontations.

Geography: Scandinavia, United States

Locations: Places of worship, banks, street preacher corners, monasteries or cloisters, museums, retirement homes.

V. The Hierophant Reversed

Overview: When Hierophant is in reverse, you may be overextending yourself and not protecting your energies properly. Sometimes making the right decision is not always clear, but you may need to do a bit more research to figure out the best course of action going forward. Miscommunications are possible, but making the best decision is far more important than being liked right now.

Love: You may be in a dating or relationship rut and the old ways of doing things are not cutting it anymore. Be mindful of how you communicate or make others feel so as not to alienate anyone. Remember, we have no space or time to love when we judge. Respect boundaries and honor promises.

Mind & Spirit: Spiritual justice will find a way eventually when the Hierophant is in reverse. Find a way to make time for meditation and mental health wellness in ways that become part of your weekly or daily routine.

Body: Pay attention to your health habits and routines, but don't be too rigid either. This might be an ideal time to try something new to enhance your exercise or dietary habits.

Money: You may need to work from home, provide homeschooling, or some type of in-home care for a loved one or children. Give more time and attention to your goals and follow through as needed to close chapters and make way for new opportunities. Be true to your inner wisdom even if authority figures might not agree. Gambling is not advised whatsoever at this time.

Meditations: Are you finding yourself struggling with tradition or being too rigid in your beliefs? This may be the time to buck tradition and do things in a new way.

VI. The Lovers

Overview: The Lovers indicates the presence of new choices, love, energies, and opportunities coming your way. It is also associated with relationships, whether business or interpersonal. While it's often looked at as a sign of romantic relationships, it's not always literal. The appearance of this card suggests the pursuit of a dream, even if it appears to be impossible, and that great rewards lie in the end. Like the dual nature of this card, you will also be faced with multiple choices, but also clear signs of the appropriate path ahead. This may also indicate a battle between mind and heart, where our emotions and logic are at odds over the right choice. In any case, this card suggests that you follow your passions and do not let fear stand in your way.

Love: When this card appears, it suggests new love and sexual energies are ahead or present. This could also mean the start of a new relationship or business venture that has long-term potential.

Mind & Spirit: You could be experiencing a spiritual partnership with someone who could aid you in achieving your spiritual goals. While this card suggests that you should follow your passions, it's important to not enter into partnerships or mentorships lightly, and to use rational thought to guide you to your objectives.

Body: You may need to work with a medical practitioner, specialist, or wellness coach to achieve your health and wellness goals. If you are facing health challenges, know that the right partner to help you get back to wholeness will come to you.

Money: Be careful not to lose track of your financial and/or professional priorities. Beware of partaking in a workplace romance but if you decide to proceed, it's imperative to understand potential consequences.

Travel: Options for travel open up, but the clear choice among many will be a place where lasting connections will be most fruitful.

Geography: East Asia, Uruguay, Bolivia, Oceania, Australia

Locations: Patisseries, candy stores, romantic locations, florists, charming cafés, or a loved one's home.

VI. The Lovers Reversed

Overview: When the Lovers are reversed, you may be facing a difficult decision, but not making a choice will leave you in an undesirable position. While the card is still generally positive even in reverse, it is also a sign of general indecision. Perhaps too many choices are causing you feel overwhelmed and unmoved out of fear. Indecision appears to be a bigger problem than making a choice. This is also a sign not to scatter your energies or overextend yourself in personal matters. Be clear about your personal relationship objectives and do not ignore your intuition.

Love: This card in reverse is still a positive sign. You might experience ambivalence regarding multiple choices or possibilities ahead. Do not allow fear to lead you to stagnation. Making a move, no matter how scary, is still far better than making no moves at all. You may also experience delays in personal matters and events that are close to the heart.

Mind & Spirit: This card in reserve cautions against developing romantic ties with mentors or people who are meant to guide you on platonic journeys. Exercise the appropriate boundaries in seeking spiritual or mental health guidance and maintain focus on your goals.

Body: Self-care is of the utmost importance now as well as loving yourself much better. This card reversed means much of the love and affection you give others should be directed at your overall wellness. If you need guidance, make contact with a professional who could help meet your wellness goals.

Money: This card in reverse means that your romantic interests may be overshadowing your priorities. This is not a time to put your work, finances, or network on the back burner. Try not to mix workplace issues with romantic ones. Think of as many potential consequences as possible before acting upon any desires that could be seen as crossing any boundaries. Be professional and mindful of your finances.

Meditations: Are you too engaged in something or not enough? Are you taking the time to smell the flowers and enjoy life's everyday pleasures? Are you cooperating with others enough?

VII. The Chariot

Overview: This card is about finding freedom from the constraints of cultural and community expectations. The number four is also a powerful sign. The energy of this card, in one word, is *movement*. It's important to be intentional with your manifestations at this time and to be disciplined in physical and spiritual energies. Taking control of any out-of-control emotions is key at this time, as well as focusing on a new path ahead. When you summon the courage to embark upon a new journey, you also discover our personal power and the freedom to be your authentic self.

Love: New journeys toward or with ones you love are ahead. Sexual energies may be a leading force at this time but be wary of letting your senses do all the driving. Be sure to define your own boundaries and expectations with others and communicate them clearly.

Mind & Spirit: Magic, divination, astral travel. Taming sexual energies and erratic emotions are part of your path, and there may be actual physical travel involved as part of your inner spiritual quest. Now is the time to explore conferences that are focused on the metaphysical, and don't be afraid of getting creative with your learning style. If you take a chance in stepping even a little outside of your comfort zone, you're likely to discover everlasting changes and deep, spiritual insights.

Body: Self-discipline – both physical and mental. Your energies are likely to be strong, so examine new fitness regimens to improve your health. You're likely to make plenty of progress if you invest in your overall wellness.

Money: Be cognizant of energies working for you or against you. Try not to dwell on doubts about investments or professional decisions – your instincts are a driving force, and the truth will come out in the wash. Your motivation to advance in your financial and professional goals are a driving force for your success. Any investments involving transportation are likely to be fortuitous as well as the ability to resolve any lingering debts. Be disciplined and mindful, and you will find success.

Travel: New journeys and finding new balance in life are afoot. Allow your energy and passion to guide you toward new horizons that fulfill your mind and heart.

Geography: Asia

Locations: Airports, train stations, highways, racetracks, garages, travel agencies, or automobile dealerships.

VII: The Chariot Reversed

Overview: The Chariot in reverse indicates that there is an imbalance in energies, efforts, partnerships, or projects. Don't waste your efforts or energies. A lack of self-discipline, whether in progress or emotions, is indicated here. Movement is still a key term even in the reversed position, and such movement is likely to be type that comes from within. Reconsider the path that you're on. Are you heading in the direction you really want to go? Or are you wasting your time?

Love: Are you using your sexual energies appropriately? Now is the time to reconsider how you've been approaching love and relationships in general. If a relationship feels stagnant, this card indicates that it's time to stop spinning your wheels and move forward in communicating your wants and needs. Find a healthy balance in your approach toward romantic partnerships. Whether you feel an extreme in enthusiasm or a depletion of it, it's time to gain more perspective and try a bit of diplomacy instead of bold assertiveness.

Mind & Spirit: Creativity requires movement, but you might be feeling stuck and held back by ego, insecurity, and doubt. Put your ego aside and exercise compassion with yourself and others. Ensure your movement in life is aligned with your purpose, allowing all that is unaligned to fall away. When you take the time to invest in our spiritual and mental wellness, you will find the answers at the times you need them. Beware of being over-enthusiastic about any new spiritual or mental health programs or advisers. Place your trust in your Higher Self and intuition rather than handing over the reins to others.

Body: Try not to overdo any new fitness regimens or overexert yourself in any activity. You might want to see quick progress regarding your physical health, but this comes with discipline and showing up consistently for yourself.

Money: When it comes to your profession and finances, be careful of being too aggressive in pushing for what you want. Not everyone around you is on the same page, so it's important to communicate your goals and objectives. This is also a time to seek counsel from subject matter experts in matters of work and money. Pump the breaks and get some perspective. Your intuition may be leading you to second-guess a decision, and you're probably right.

Meditations: Is there a need for you or someone else to have a change of heart and/or mind? Are you feeling held down or refusing to assert yourself when needed? Are you refusing to acknowledge your own movement and progress to date?

VIII: Strength

Overview: The Strength card indicates the strength of your will as it comes from your Higher Self. It's about harnessing wild passions and energies and having the discipline to use your power wisely. This is not a time to force progress, but a time of gentleness, diplomacy, compassion, and patience. New births, whether literal or metaphorical, are indicated as well as taking care of or helping young ones around you.

Love: The beast within (ego) is tamed through the strength of the Divine Feminine within our Higher Self. While this is not the time for confrontation, don't hesitate to respond assertively when needed. This is a generally positive card for love and mutually beneficial partnerships, and a great time to meet new people if that's part of your path.

Mind & Spirit: This is a time for introspection. This is not a time to fight or argue for the sake of it, but to be mindful of how you approach others and your own needs. New expressions of your own personal power are highlighted along with an emergence of creativity and intuitive powers. Mind over matter is key with the Strength card, so it's important to overcome any doubts or fears in pursuit of fulfilling your purpose. This is a time of introspection and focusing on what's important. You are stronger and more powerful than you think. Self-compassion is key.

Body: Strength of will and speed is key for your wellness. This is a great time to address breaking any vices and creating reasonable wellness goals for yourself. This is an auspicious time for your health and wellness.

Money: Financial and professional endeavors are likely to go well and don't be afraid to seek compensation for your skill and hard work. You deserve it! This might also be a great time to think of entrepreneurial pursuits that fit your personal and professional goals. While you may be considering a larger investment or purchase, be sure you have a reasonable plan for the path ahead. It's okay to be excited about investing or spending, but do not be reckless about it either.

Travel: Travel for the sake of taking care of others or the self is highlighted here. Feminine energies guide the way forward.

Geography: Africa, Australia, Asia

Locations: Fitness centers, martial arts studios, salons, zoos, or animal sanctuaries.

VIII: Strength Reversed

Overview: When Strength appears in reverse, you may be trying to assert yourself in situations that call for more diplomacy and less force. Be careful of being too aggressive, controlling, rigid or otherwise difficult in situations that are calling for patience and collaboration. Failure to strike a balance will result in unnecessary complications. You're strong, so give yourself and others credit where it's merited. Gratitude can help change your perspective or that of others around you.

Love: The reversed meaning of the Strength card is still quite positive for love. Whether single or in a relationship, this is a great time for quality time and communicating each other's goals, dreams, and passions. However, maintain healthy boundaries and try not to look at others through rose-colored lenses.

Mind & Spirit: This is not a time to lose your nerve or surrender – nor is it a time to be overly aggressive. If you're having trouble assessing your own strengths and areas to develop, seek the counsel of a trusted friend or adviser. This is also a time to consider spending time outdoors to connect with your Divine Feminine energies rooted in Mother Nature. Be present in the power of earth's energy, as connecting to it will remind you of your highest self and purpose.

Body: While health is predicted to be generally good at this time, be sure not to overdo any wellness goals or to address your health with any quick-fixes. Any harsh decisions are likely to have a negative outcome.

Money: Be sure not to overdo any aspect of financial or professional endeavors. Proceed with caution and avoid any get-rich-quick schemes. Re-examine what your long-term goals are and what truly motivates you before deciding. Take your time. There is strength in patience.

Meditations: How can you best show up in support for others or your community? Are you working smarter or harder? Do you need to be cautious about who has access to your ideas, projects, or resources? Don't try to do everything on your own or think it has to be your way or the highway. Sometimes we best achieve our objectives by being open to hearing helpful feedback and open to introspection.

IX: The Hermit

Overview: The Hermit is a card of profound introspection and spiritual insight. Through silent wisdom, vision, and guidance, you may best fulfill your purpose by going within. Hermit is also a symbol of spiritual mastery, prophetic visions, and manifesting through your own inner magic. In this time, you may be noticing subtle signs, cues, and omens you might have missed before. You'll be more attuned to picking up on the undercurrents of others and their true intentions that are not always spoken in words. You may also notice subtle slips of the tongue in conversations that reveal a person's true intent, and it's important that you trust your gut feelings when you sense something might be off about a person or situation.

Love: When doing what's right in your love life, be sure that you have your wants and needs considered as well. The Hermit showing up in the context of love indicates that your inner voice and boundaries matter, too. This is also an omen of a possible love reunion from your past, but have you learned your lessons from this person since you had last met? If this or any relationship doesn't align with your Higher Self, reconsider the romance. This may be a time for you to fall in love with you rather than distracting yourself with someone else. If you're already in a relationship, this may be time to get creative in spicing things up.

Mind & Spirit: When you trust your intuition and silent impressions, you allow the heightening of your senses to analyze everything around you. In doing so, you remind yourself of the interconnectedness of our Universe. Aggressively and quietly pursue the passions connecting you to your Higher Self. When you learn to trust your inner voice, your wisdom becomes harnessed to make manifestation magic. It's time to go within and spend time learning about your shadow self. You'll find intense clarity at night and in your dream state.

Body: Focusing on your health is advised at this time, especially as it relates to gastrointestinal issues and mental health conditions. Take some needed time for self-care, even if it's sitting in your living room reading a fun book or simply doing nothing at all. Some of the stress you may be feeling can manifest into physical symptoms, so make time for your wellness or be prepared to make time for an illness. Issues of hearing and sight are also important to bear in mind at this time.

Money: Don't be afraid to ask for help if you're feeling all alone in your finances or professional goals. If you need to get organized and reexamine your priorities, this is a great time to do so. Ensure you are acting with integrity in any financial or professional decisions regardless of who may notice, and you will surely see the advantageous results in the end. This is a time of prudence and caution when it comes to spending or investing.

Travel: You may travel to seek the guidance of a subject matter expert or to spend some quality alone time. You'll find that a change of location, especially one with a high elevation, provides a wonderful new perspective.

Geography: Africa, Peru, Ecuador, Venezuela, North America

Locations: High elevations, mountainous terrain, caves, rural areas, cenotes, spiritual retreats, lighthouses, forest cottages, remote retreat centers, libraries, and isolated regions.

IX: The Hermit Reversed

Overview: The Hermit in reverse is still a card of deep introspection and following your true spiritual journey. Spending too much time in isolation or surrounded by others might be taking its toll on your psyche, so don't be afraid of asking for help when you need it most. There is strength in needing others. No one is an island.

Love: You might be questioning a reunion from the past and if it aligns with your needs. Is what the other person is saying adding up to the vibe they're giving you? Trust your quiet wisdom and go within. Be careful of resisting wise words, whether of trusted loved ones or your inner voice, as you may need to take a step back and observe before acting. If you're already in a relationship, be sure you're not spending too much time in your own head and be present and attentive with those you love.

Mind & Spirit: Are you taking your quest for introspection a bit too far or enjoying isolation a bit more than you should? While nurturing yourself is imperative, do not use it to escape responsibilities or meaningful interactions with others. When we are coming from a place of authenticity and vulnerability, we are also aligning with our Higher Self.

Body: When the Hermit appears in reverse, it may be time for an upgrade in your fitness and wellness plans. Shake off the dust that's been collecting in routine monotony and try something new and exciting to give yourself a boost of vitality. Meaningful changes to your health can take time but be patient. With hard work and discipline as well as new approaches, you're likely to see wonderful changes.

Money: Communication is key to clearing up any financial or professional misunderstandings. Observe, ask questions as needed, and reflect before making any major decisions. Seek the counsel of others if you're experiencing any doubts about the path forward. If you're going to spend time alone, do so while brushing up on a skill or learning a new one. This is not a time to be frivolous in your spending, and a financial adviser could prove invaluable.

Meditations: Are you ignoring your intuition? Are you communicating our intentions properly? Are you paying attention to the symbols and themes of your dreams? Are you paying enough attention to what is said and unsaid in conversations or are you being complacent? Are you ignoring wise advice? Go after your goals quietly, but after you've weighed all the pros and cons with logic and reason.

X: Wheel of Fortune

Overview: The Wheel of Fortune is ruled by Saturn and indicates heeding your inner voice and trusting in the natural cycles of change. While change can be seen on the spectrum of positive or negative, it's important to view changes as a natural part of life. In late fall or early winter, you may encounter a significant change to your present circumstances. This may be a time to anticipate changes through your own physical or psychological "spring cleaning." Expect changes or projects in 2s or 3s. When we resist new chapters, we can sometimes bring more pain upon ourselves. The Wheel of Fortune is ruled by Jupiter and is here to remind you that things are happening in its own time and that change is inevitable. To see the greatest rewards and success in upcoming change, you must adapt to the new cycle.

Love: Changes to your love life are on the horizon. If you're in a relationship, it's time to address any needed changes or to simply try new things to reinvigorate your partnership. If you're seeking a relationship, set your intentions on all your wants and needs before starting anything new. Positive changes happen if you're intentional and clear about it. Stasis is lethal to romance.

Mind & Spirit: The Wheel of Fortune isn't just about changes to the physical realm, but also the spiritual and psychological. This is an invitation to explore the shadow self and the workings of the subconscious mind. Don't try to do things along someone else's timeline, but your own and when you're ready. Taking time to give gratitude and enjoy the sweetness of life is also highly recommended. Now is not the time to be a martyr.

Body: Be mindful of sugar intake as well as your sleep cycle. You might not like the health advice you get soon, but you may need to make changes for the better for your overall wellness. Instead of being obstinate or complaining, be proactive in taking care of your physical and mental health.

Money: Professional projects or financial opportunities come in 2s or 3s. Major changes could be seen in your professional life and if you've always wondered what it would be like to change professions or go after a dream, now is the time. Seek mentorship in areas where you want to excel, and you may find that your ambitions can be realized with the help of someone who possesses the insight you've needed all along. If you've been in a tough spot financially, look forward to a turn for the better soon, but know that successes and failures should be looked at as temporary – change is always on the horizon. Saving money or setting aside an emergency stash is highly advised.

Travel: Abrupt changes in travel plans or surprise journeys are on the horizon.

Geography: Suriname, Guyana, North America, Australia

Locations: Ferris wheels, carnivals, casinos, stock exchange, roundabouts, nightclubs. Or places that sell lottery tickets.

X: Wheel of Fortune Reversed

Overview: The Wheel of Fortune is ruled by Saturn and is a card for inevitable change in any position, but this position indicates that it's not only time to pay attention to natural cycles of change, but to also reflect upon whether you're heeding the call of your inner voice. This reversal may indicate you might be allowing external circumstances or other people to dictate your direction while ignoring your own cycles and instincts. This is not a time to hide away from the world, but a time to address what may be the root cause of your irritation. All that is not in alignment with your Higher Self must fall away.

Love: You might find yourself feeling irritable with your partner or love life in general. When you ignore our needs and desires, you can sometimes project that discomfort onto others when you should be addressing it yourself. Do not ignore your inner voice when it comes to love. If a relationship has run its course, be honest with yourself about it and communicate your intentions clearly to others involved.

Mind & Spirit: Spend time contemplating your growth. This is time to spend tending to a garden and reflecting upon changes you've encountered throughout the course of your life. Give yourself credit for all that you've accomplished and overcome. New opportunities are on their way.

Body: Pay extra attention to your blood work, kidneys, and other filtration organs. If your diet consists of too much sugar, this might be the time to reduce intake. Pay attention to how stress affects your health and wellness. Make conscious choices about your health and from a place of personal power instead of a place of defensiveness. This is not a time to challenge the advice of your doctor.

Money: This is a time to make decisions that are aligned with our true purpose and long-term goals. Change is en route regarding finances and/or vocation, but you must make difficult decisions that are based on your alignment rather than the expectations of others. Be prepared for worst-case and best-case scenarios. If a decision doesn't make sense, what's the point? Something is about to shake things up out of your normal routine or planning, so get ready.

Meditations: Are you ignoring your inner voice? Do you feel like your judgment has been off lately? Are you dishing out or receiving a lot of criticism? It's time to go within and figure out what's not fulfilling you. Go with the flow of the cycles of change and trust that things will work out in due time.

XI: Justice

Overview: Justice indicates the powers of cause and effect are at play. Its appearance signifies an important decision has been made. Justice will be given out in the situation around us and we must learn our lessons in order to avoid repeating mistakes. This card also indicates fortitude, community solidarity, or mourning the loss of a loved one. It may also reflect a decision made where intersectional aspects of identity were considered. Justice is on the way, and it's time to trust in your own judgment as well. Honesty, integrity, and truth are paramount. As we are all connected with one another, it's important to seek a life of balance interpersonally and with ourselves.

Love: Loyalty and affection are often indicated with Justice. However, you may also need to turn your attention to what your significant other is doing and be fair in all matters of the heart. Do your best to create and maintain a household where everyone is heard and participates in chores as well as fun activities. Harmony is key, and if that doesn't exist, it's time to make a decision. If you're looking for a relationship, write your intentions and what you desire in a partner. The sooner you indicate what you want and need, the sooner the Universe can deliver.

Mind & Spirit: Trusting your intuition in terms of what feels right rather than relying on words alone is the theme of Justice. Practice mindfulness and remember that being present can help you achieve balance.

Body: Senses of sight and smell may be affected. Discipline in doing the right thing by your health is indicated, and that involves maintaining a healthy balance in diet, exercise, and overall wellness.

Money: Act with integrity in your work environment; justice is on the way. Motivation and discipline in finances and/or vocation are highly suggested as well as keeping an eye out for a sudden increase in your bank account. Be mindful of balancing your professional and personal life.

Travel: Traveling in 3s or as a larger group is recommended. You may be on your way to resolve legal matters or to settle a dispute.

Geography: North Africa, Southern Europe, North America

Locations: Courts, attorney offices, law enforcement agencies, mediation/arbitration offices, tax consultant offices, or places where exams for licensing occur.

XI: Justice Reversed

Overview: Justice in reverse usually indicates a loss due to external factors or a sense of disempowerment on your side. While there are many factors in life that we can't control that can leave us feeling we're living with ongoing injustice, it's important to remember that we can control how we respond – or not. This doesn't mean justice eludes you, but that events will play out in the time that it's meant to and worrying is futile.

Love: There may be a sense of disharmony within your current relationship or a sense of injustice in your love life in general. This is a time to reflect upon how you may be contributing to your own unhappiness, and how much anyone else is accountable for it. Reflect, then communicate your boundaries instead of disappearing into a partnership. Meditate on what you need and never lose sight of your sense of self.

Mind & Spirit: Direct your energies to resolving any outstanding issues instead of worrying and fretting. If you've forgotten your importance in this world, your higher purpose, now is the time to reflect on where imbalances exist and address them accordingly.

Body: Take care of any sensory issues at this time, especially if you're experiencing any issues with sight or your sense of smell. Moderation is key in all aspects of your wellness regimen.

Money: Beware of legal troubles, frivolous gambling, or neglecting debts. This is a time to be proactive and mindful in financial and vocational matters. If you're facing difficulties in your workplace, be mindful of what you can and can't control, and don't make and rash decisions. Take logical steps to resolve disputes or debts as needed and avoid allowing emotions to take the wheel. If you're waiting on a loan, there may be delays.

Meditations: Are you being too individualistic and ignoring the needs of others around you? Are you repeating past mistakes? Are you trusting your instincts? Have you been responding to people or events as needed? How are you responding to a current injustice?

XII: The Hanged Man

Overview: The Hanged Man is ruled by Neptune and signifies changes in perspective. New perceptions and opportunities are about to appear, and truths will be uncovered as a result. Creative ideas will flow through, and you'll see situations and people in brand new ways. This is a time where you're deciding between a few major decisions, and instead of rushing toward any, that it's better to see things from as many angles as possible. Instead of trying to control or manipulate a situation, take a step back and observe. You'll find hidden messages in the words and actions of others as well as what's not being said. Let go of anything that isn't serving your best interests. Trust your intuition as unexpected views and outcomes are about to manifest.

Love: Pay attention to what's being said – or not – in conversations about love. Instead of reacting, pause and center yourself. Does something feel strange about the situation? Does the vibe feel a bit different? Sometimes people are not going to be as forthcoming as you like, and you can either inquire or sit back and observe. Sometimes we get the answers we seek not by asking questions but paying attention to all that's unsaid. Let go of anything (outdated thinking, ideas, etc.) or anyone who may be hurting you. If everything feels fine for you, be sure to check in on how your significant other is feeling – and what they might be doing when you're not looking.

Mind & Spirit: It's imperative to not just be mindful, but to release any negativity. You are more in control of your destiny than you realize and are holding the pen for your next chapter. Proceed in being proactive and take charge of your future.

Body: You might be second-guessing a diagnosis or health condition after a change in perspective or new information. Be open to treatment options and communicate your concerns with your healthcare provider.

Money: This is a time to reflect and relax in order to make the right decision. If things feel stagnant, then it's probably time to try something new. However, don't be quick to jump ship. Take your time in evaluating your needs and long-term goals and proceed accordingly. Be open to things going well financially and sharing with others when experiencing abundance.

Travel: New horizons are about to manifest as you navigate new terrain. You may take a journey to mourn the loss of a leader, mentor, or adviser.

Geography: South America (especially Ecuador)

Locations: Adrenaline sports locations, bridges, or skyscrapers.

XII: The Hanged Man Reversed

Overview: When the Hanged Man is in reverse, you may be failing to rise above a situation. While change can be painful, it's important to remember that such discomfort is fleeting and temporary. Nothing is forever, and you only hurt yourself by hanging on to situations or ideas that are no longer beneficial. If you're unsure of how to move forward, perhaps it's best to not make a move at all and gain perspective before making any choices. This is not a time to try to control anything, but to allow things to flow in and out naturally. When we align with our Higher Self, things work out as they need to.

Love: Someone who is a loner or in disguise is suggested here. Let go of outdated thinking when it comes to love. Don't hang onto the status quo. Take a break and get some perspective on romance and what it means to both love and be loved. If you find yourself standing at a romantic crossroads, give yourself time to think and feel your way through. Pay attention to subtle signs, nonverbal cues, and hidden motives.

Mind & Spirit: It's time to face your fears. Let go and try something new.

Body: Hearing issues may be affecting you or related to an ongoing problem. It may be time to get another opinion on your health and be sure you're heard in all your concerns, but receptive to the answers as well. It may be time to adjust your health habits and be mindful of psychosomatic symptoms.

Money: Accountability is key at work and in matters of money. Before pointing any fingers at anyone, ask yourself how you might have contributed to an undesirable situation. Face your fears and challenge your perspective. If your situation isn't ideal, then it's time to consider other options. Get professional assistance and advice as needed instead of trying to figure out everything alone.

Meditations: Outdated beliefs and mindsets may be causing stress or harm at this time. Are you refusing to see the truth because it makes you uncomfortable? Is 'better the devil you know than the one you don't' a good approach or a comfort zone? Are you letting your imagination get the best of you, or is logic being used? Are you seeing the forest for the trees?

XIII: Death

Overview: The Death card is not one that merely indicates a physical death, but rather the shedding of the old self, ego, patterns, and making way for rebirth. Themes of overcoming, healing, the cycle of life, death, and rebirth are all present in this card. When this card appears, we make way for the new and allow the flow of a natural cycle. The power of transformation and shedding old skin is underway. Transitions can be difficult, but change is inevitable so it's imperative to do your best to adapt. With every beginning, there's an ending.

Love: Changes that transform your love life are happening – for better or worse. People or situations you might've counted on before might not be there any longer. Release any remaining fears and beware of resisting change. Don't rely on what you see or hear alone – go within and trust what you're feeling. Be clear and direct in your communication and make rational decisions. If you do nothing, someone else will be deciding for you.

Mind & Spirit: This is a time of opening up new spiritual realms, whether it's lucid dreaming or spirit guides. You'll notice a heightened sensitivity to spiritual activity around you, making you extra sensitive to the vibrations of people, places, and circumstances. New sources of creativity, wisdom, and personal power are appearing before you. Use your gifts wisely. Resisting change is not advised, and when you open yourself to a new chapter, you might find that change was desperately needed after all.

Body: Change and healing is underway after a transformation. If you've outgrown certain ways of living, it's time for a significant adjustment or a major change will happen for you. Stress may lead to self-medicating with vices, which is highly cautioned. Be up front about what you need to make your life better. Make your destiny, don't wait for it to come to you.

Money: When it comes to a professional situation, it's time to decide on a new path or a major one will happen for you. Dislike your job? Make some moves now or find yourself fired or laid off. Change is inevitable, whether it's money or your vocation. Difficult decisions may need to be made regarding finances that lead to cutbacks, losses, or struggles. Be brave in dealing with situations immediately and don't be afraid to ask for help.

Travel: You may embark on a journey to close a chapter in life. This could be for a death, memorial, or to finalize a major life change.

Geography: South America (Peru especially)

Locations: Morgue, cemetery, funeral home, disaster sites, or memorials.

XIII: Death Reversed

Overview: Death in reverse tends to indicate that there are things happening around you and that the truth is a bit hard to swallow. You might also be overstimulated, overwhelmed, or taking on too much at this time. Positive change can happen when you take your time to do things mindfully and with clear intentions. This is a time of personal transformation, and the shedding of old ideas and situations that are no longer meant to be part of your story.

Love: This is not a time to sleepwalk through your love life or friendships. Be mindful and proactive in addressing all matters of the heart and conversations that need to be had. Are you lashing out at those you love when you could be calmly telling them what's really going on with you? Instead of slowly pulling off the bandage, it might be better to swiftly remove it and be real about the wounds as well as the need to heal. If someone is unhappy, it needs to be said. And if it's time to let go, then let go. Dragging things out or phoning the relationship in is not recommended. Getting a professional to mediate is highly advised.

Mind & Spirit: If you find yourself in over your head, it's time to not only step back but to examine your own outlook on the situation. Are you failing to act or doing too much at once? Find the sense of balance that is appropriate for you. Know that the heartache you're feeling is temporary and allow yourself to process – just don't unpack and permanently live in your sorrow. It's time to face your fears. Connect with a trusted contact or professional for advice.

Body: Be mindful of psychosomatic symptoms and how your physical health is being impacted by stress. Talk with a professional and consider ways you could be proactive in your self-care. You deserve a break, and perhaps you need a change of pace to give you the perspective you need to move forward on a healthier path.

Money: If you're dissatisfied in work and/or financial prospects, know that this era is temporary. You might consider making a career change at this time or making a major shift in your income streams. This is the time for major changes, and it's better if you're actively participating in the process than passively accepting circumstances.

Meditations: Are you refusing to make or accept changes? Are you trying to force or avoid a situation that requires your attention? Are you hanging onto what no longer belongs in your story? There are opportunities to heal, don't ignore the chances for meaningful transformation.

XIV: Temperance

Overview: Temperance is a card that deals with new realms, possibilities, and harmony. It is a card of softening and thoughtful moderation in pursuit of balance. Now is the time to cleanse oneself of dusty, negative mindsets to make way for a time of harmony and listening to your inner voice. Winter is a period where the dreamworld will lend you more clues about the path ahead – pay attention. Any new ideas, opportunities, or projects that begin during winter should have follow-through thereafter. You may be making plans to travel soon.

Love: Diplomacy and balance in relationships are key now. There's no need to panic or rush into any major decisions. Seek harmony and use compassion in all matters of the heart. Before you can share your love with others, be sure that you're loving yourself first. One cannot pour from an empty cup. Release regrets, fears, and worries.

Mind & Spirit: You may be experiencing a heightened sensitivity to the feelings of others as well as yourself. Have patience and focus on balancing your emotions as well as your responses. This is a wonderful time for meditation and trusting your intuition for guidance. This is a card for introspection.

Body: Mindful use of your energy is vital as well as self-control. Examine your overall fitness and wellness. If anything feels out of balance, be sure to address it soon.

Money: You may be taking a new course or learning a new skill for personal and/or business development. Ensure you're making decisions based on your best interests rather than from the ego. Evaluate your long-term goals and plans. Do those plans align with your Higher Self? Have patience in workplace/professional issues as your hard work isn't going unnoticed. This is a good time for balancing your finances as well as increasing wealth.

Travel: Long-distance travel (foreign or domestic) away from your home. Trips to summits, conferences, or courses.

Geography: South America

Locations: Breweries, bars, waterfront homes, waterfalls, sources of water, family home, or waiting rooms.

XIV: Temperance Reversed

Overview: Impatience, imprudence, and disharmony in personal, spiritual, and/or physical wellness. Overindulging in vices and allowing the physical and material to take precedence. This is not a time to force anything – or else it will be met with disaster and loss. If you're avoiding your issues, as well as the concerns of others, it's time to address what's holding you back from being your best self. If you're unsure about what to do in a situation, you may likely see the results or the right answer by the end of winter.

Love: An indication of misusing sexual energies or manipulating loved ones. Allowing passions and tempers to flare out of control could prove disastrous. Imbalances in love of others as well as the self. The quest for wholeness is not dependent on finding others to fill a void for you but addressing that void yourself. You can attract the right circumstances and people when you've done the work for yourself first.

Mind & Spirit: The ego is emphasized rather than the Higher Self in this position. Energy vampirism and external factors provide drains on the psyche. This is not a time to ignore the Higher Self. If you're in need of assistance, reach out to a trusted friend, loved one, or a professional. A loss of faith in oneself and trust in the Universe.

Body: Ensure that you're getting enough sleep as well as paying attention to our dreams. Symptoms may manifest as a result of a lack of self-care.

Money: Cooperation is key to making professional or financial progress. You may find that hyper-individualism is not helpful in making meaningful or lasting changes. Imbalances in finances can be addressed with use of moderation in spending and making mindful decisions about money. This is not a time to be passive professionally as this position indicates a need for a proactive and tempered approach in evaluating your worth as well as seeking compensation.

Meditations: What's holding you back from being your best self? Are you potentially trying to rush ahead on plans before maturation? Are you not looking before you leap? Things take time, and beautiful results can manifest with patience.

XV: The Devil

Overview: While the Devil may appear to be an intimidating figure, its appearance shines a light on the ways we keep ourselves imprisoned to vices, materialism, and overindulgence of all varieties. In a traditional tarot deck, you might find that the Devil appears to have enslaved two humans. However, when you examine the illustration closer, you see that the chains around their necks are quite loose – loose enough to escape if they wished. It is their own ego that binds them and prevents them from ascending to their Higher Selves. When the Devil appears, we must ask ourselves if we're allowing ourselves to be held back by material or physical greed or going overboard with any destructive habits. You have a choice. Decide upon a path toward wellness or continue to live in the prison of your own making. It's completely up to you to take that first step to regain control of your life.

Love: Someone – perhaps you – may be feeling bound to the relationship in an unhealthy way. Someone may prefer to continue with romantic illusions instead of seeing the writing on the wall. This is not a time to be overindulgent or complacent in your relationship, so be proactive and look at the entire situation with a rational lens. Is someone unhappy? Is the spark dying out? Is someone taking bad habits to an extreme? It's time to talk about it. If you're single, examine your attitude toward relationships. Are you indulging in superficial physical pleasures to escape real intimacy? Are you running away from being honest about how you truly feel? You may be guilty of self-sabotage, but remember that you deserve to be truly happy, to be genuinely loved and to have the freedom to love someone back. Sometimes taking a little time to figure out what you truly want it what's best before looking for love.

Mind & Spirit: Are you keeping toxic company or false friends who are bringing out the worst in you? It may be time to reconsider your friends circle and evaluate if they're who you want accompanying you through your life. Are they cheering for your success? Or are they using you, berating you, or hindering you in any way? This is a time to align with your Higher Self and don't be afraid to shed the chains of what may be weighing you down. You are free to walk away from drama, toxic people, and unhealthy situations. We are responsible for what we accomplish as well as the company we keep.

Body: Beware of overdoing anything whether the habit is healthy or destructive. This is a time to contemplate whether you're pushing yourself too hard or not at all, or if you're engaging in risky behavior without thinking of long-term consequences. Too much stress, strain, or fatigue may be taking its toll on your body if you're not careful. If you're trying to manage long-term illnesses, pain, or addictions, remember that you are not alone. Reach out for help and support as needed. You have more power than you realize!

Money: You may feel as though you have limited control of your finances and/or our professional path. Desires for professional or financial success may come at a cost if you're not cognizant of the entire situation. This may be a time of great sacrifice to get what you want. Remember that the decision you make will be one of free will, and you will have no one to blame but yourself. Decide if the path ahead of you is one worth the risks and rewards. Be sure to monitor your spending and create a budget if necessary. This is not a time to gamble with your future and ask for guidance as needed.

Travel: You may be taking a journey where you'll have the potential for elevating your social status or indulging in vices. Weigh the pros and cons of your decisions and choose wisely.

Geography: Oceania, Caribbean, Uruguay, North Africa

Locations: Casinos, strip clubs, bars, sex worker sites, sex shops, liquor stores, nightclubs, or any place where vices could be exploited.

XV: The Devil Reversed

Overview: The Devil in reverse is undoubtedly an auspicious position as it indicates taking control of your destiny. Ready to shed destructive habits? The time is now, and success is indeed possible – but you must be proactive about it. An overall decrease in selfishness, greed, jealousy, and all inclinations that truly hold you back from ascending to be your best is on the horizon. This is about getting real with who you are and everyone around you. This is a great time to regain control of your creative abilities as well as your daily routine. You're ready to shed the veil of illusion so you can see your path to enlightenment with eyes wide open.

Love: While you may feel a bit out of control in romantic relationships, this is an indication that you're willing to see beyond the illusions and superficial appearances. Take each step in your love life with grace, intent, and mindfulness. If you're feeling bound to a romantic relationship in any way, deal with your doubts immediately and with a rational mindset. If you feel like your romantic options are limited, realize that you are more in control of your destiny than you imagine. Love yourself first, genuinely, and when the time is right, you can invite someone else to love you, too. When you project an air of desperation, you make yourself vulnerable to toxic partners. When you come from a place of true self-love – not superficial bravado – you can see love without rose-colored lenses and decide if someone is truly worth your time and energy.

Mind & Spirit: Are you speaking up as much as you should? Are you being inconsiderate in your communication? Now is the time to examine where you are emotionally and see how you can make positive changes. Maintaining a positive attitude is key at this time as well as keeping a network of supportive friends or family. No matter what your current limitations are, you have way more power than you think and can start your path to freedom.

Body: Beware of overextending yourself in any way and recognize your limitations within reason. You can aim for improvement, but don't hurt yourself in the process.

Money: Be mindful of employment opportunities or financial decisions that may not guarantee long-term success. Look beyond the superficial aspects and get as much information as you can to make an informed decision. If you're currently unhappy with your financial status or profession, start looking into ways you can change that. Otherwise, you may be trapping yourself in a prison of your own making.

Meditations: Do you have a distorted picture of how life is supposed to be? Is it time to re-evaluate your priorities? Are you communicating your needs? Have you lost sight of your Higher Self? Are you letting other people influence your decision-making or are you choosing to align with your authentic self?

XVI: The Tower

Overview: The Tower card, like the Devil or Death, can be quite intimidating or frightening, but they are reminders of the cycle of life, death, and rebirth. When the Tower appears, change is about to occur abruptly so be on your guard and prepare as much as you can. It's time to release the past and tear down old beliefs, habits, and ways of life to make way for the new. No matter what difficulties you face in life, remember that change is imminent and that better is possible. While change can be scary or shocking, know that those feelings are temporary. Do your best to remain flexible. You might not be able to rely on people, places, or things that you once did, and clinging to outdated modes of living will be to your detriment. It is ruled by Mars.

Love: This may be a sign that a romantic connection or long-term relationship is about to experience a shock. Maybe it's a bit of truth someone may have been hiding that comes to light? Maybe things are about to come to an end? This is a time to be proactive in matters of the heart and not wait for the construct of love to come crashing down. Don't sleep on any doubts. If you're looking for love, this may be a time to take a step back and be cognizant about what you really want. Love shouldn't be painful.

Mind & Spirit: If you've been getting high on fantasy, be prepared for a harsh dose of reality. While it's important to have goals and dreams, it's also important to be realistic about your priorities.

Body: Health issues pertaining to eyesight and sense of smell are indicated. Excessive stress may be affecting your health so it may be time to consider how you can manage your overall wellness. Also, beware of substance misuse.

Money: This is not a time to lose your cool when it comes to money or work. There may be instability ahead when it comes to your finances and/or professional life. Making wise decisions now with a level head will pay off later, so avoid rash decisions. Deal with conflicts logically and directly instead of waiting for situations to explode.

Travel: Journeys to big cities with tall buildings or travel dealing with sudden losses.

Geography: Caribbean

Locations: Skyscrapers, towers, tall buildings, high places that are dangerous, mountaintops, prisons, fire departments, and haunted locations.

XVI: The Tower Reversed

Overview: Even in reverse, the Tower is about change. Trying to stop or impede changes at this time will only result in chaos. This is not the time to cling to the status quo or fair-weather allies. Gather your resources and plan as much as you can to deal with coming changes or possible emergencies. Try not to take anything personally at this time as misunderstandings are quite possible.

Love: When it comes to relationships or looking for love, this is about being more mindful of others and refraining from trying to change people. Engage in meaningful dialogue and communicate your wants and needs in a way anyone can understand. Even if you hear something you don't like, take a deep breath, and take your time in digesting the information.

Mind & Spirit: There may be ideas or ways of living that are hurting you, and it may be time to change your course immediately. You can maintain a positive attitude while being realistic. It's time to get rid of feelings of jealousy, resentment, or fear.

Body: You may be experiencing digestive issues that pertain to eating habits or are having issues "digesting" new information that's uncomfortable to hear. Be mindful of performing any tasks that can cause bodily harm.

Money: 40,000 appears to be an important number, but it's also important to not make any rash decisions with your finances or work. You may notice others behaving erratically in your field or workplace but do your best to avoid getting involved as much as possible. Take some time to process information and be mindful with your communication. This is not a time to expect a windfall – whether in money or career opportunities. Financial troubles are possible, especially if materialism could be your downfall.

Meditations: Are you hanging onto things that are no longer of any benefit to you? Is there healing you need in some aspect of your life? Are you refusing to see what's happening around you? Are you afraid to let go or impatient about current progress? Are you resisting change?

XVII: The Star

Overview: After the destruction of the Tower, the Star follows, shining brightly while indicating rebirth, enlightenment, creativity, and success. This is a time to generate new light in your life by setting new goals and opening yourself up to new opportunities. Networking and developing meaningful friendships are important as well as courage to venture down new paths. This is an ideal time to make notes of all your wonderful creative ideas. Even if you don't know how exactly to act upon those ideas, don't worry. By putting them in your notes, you activate the ideas from the realm of imagination into reality. When you unleash your creativity, you provide your own inspiration that will come in handy for long-term success. People around you may begin to reassess their perspectives and your desire to know the truth will be powerful.

Love: New opportunities in relationships or new love are indicated. Opportunities to make romantic ideas come true are imminent, so don't waste your energy with trivial nonsense. This is an optimistic time for love and relationships, whether to build something new or to rejuvenate a long-term commitment. Love or improving a current relationship won't happen on its own – you must be an active participant in making the romance magic happen. Newer, deeper levels of commitment are possible.

Mind & Spirit: Spiritual gifts are now awakening. You may be looking into new ways of learning about the mind or a new spiritual path. Have patience with yourself and trust your intuition on what feels best for you. New opportunities in emotional and spiritual wellness are indicated, especially if your gifts can be shared. Set your mind to big goals and take action!

Body: It's time to trust your own body's rhythms and investigate wellness programs that fit your physical and psychological needs. This is a great time to get new insight on how to look and feel your very best.

Money: Financial goals are likely to be met with the appearance of the Star. Exercise gratitude but get as much information as possible before making professional decisions. New opportunities will arise to improve finances and professional development. Financial risks are likely to pay off, whether it's an investment or asking for a raise.

Travel: Taking a trip to broaden your horizons from beautiful landscapes to cultural icons.

Geography: Africa, Asia, Caribbean

Locations: Art galleries, art shops, museums, theaters, planetariums, music halls, opera houses, ideal spots for stargazing, or beautiful locations near water

XVII: The Star Reversed

Overview: When the Star is in reverse, you may be experiencing a lack of inspiration or misjudgment of a situation. It's possible that you're focusing on something that doesn't need to be a priority or wandering off the path of your goals. You may also be letting others cloud your judgement. While you can be optimistic about the future, it's important to see the whole picture before making any misinformed decisions. If you're feeling pessimistic, take a moment to think about why and if it's helpful to maintain a certain mindset.

Love: An end to a friendship or long-term commitment may be cause for distress. Look for ways to bring new energy into meaningful ties with others instead of scattering your energy. When you are present, you can love. If someone seems distracted in your life, now is the time to have an honest conversation. Be real about what obstacles may exist in your love life and how you may be more accountable to your happiness as well as a current or potential partner.

Mind & Spirit: You may be feeling stuck or uninspired on your current path. If you're feeling bored or unhappy with your current situation, set new goals and make a checklist to affirm what you really want. Trying new things may be frightening, but it will prove to be a lot more beneficial than choosing to stay stuck in a rut. This is a good time to meet new people to generate inspiration and motivation. Trust your inner voice and make an effort to connect with like-minded people.

Body: Mental health issues and poor diet are key points with the Star in reverse. How is your current diet affecting you physically and emotionally?

Money: Opportunities to improve finances and your professional life might not be obvious but they are there. Ask yourself if there is anything preventing you from seeing the big picture or opportunities that are coming your way. Be mindful about those decisions and plan ahead for success. If you're not feeling great about your work environment or status, write down affirmations of what your ideal situation looks like – then take steps to make it reality.

Meditations: Are you allowing pessimism to block your vision? Are you trying to push your way down the wrong path? Are others leading you down the wrong path? Are you truly using your spiritual gifts or allowing them to stay dormant?

XVIII: The Moon

Overview: The Moon is a reminder to listen to your intuition and that not everything that's around you is as it seems. This card can indicate melancholy, saudade, or depression. This a time to pay close attention to your dreams, intuition, and emotions. However, be careful about getting lost in illusions, fantasy, or deception. If you or someone else is refusing to face the truth, this could have negative repercussions later. Secrecy, confusion, victimization, and hidden enemies are also themes of the Moon, so be sure to pay extra close attention to your own thought patterns and controlling your response to unsavory situations. Your intuition is powerful right now, but you must also remain calm and collected.

Love: You may be refusing to see deception in your romantic life. Is it better to hear the ugly truth or a beautiful lie? The choice is yours. Instead of being swayed by powerful emotions, try to take a step back and re-examine the situation. Are you seeing everything properly? What might you be missing that your intuition is potentially buzzing around? Beware of false friends, loved ones, or allies who may not have your best intentions at heart. If you get an inkling that someone is untrustworthy, you're probably right. However, refrain from assumptions and address fears and doubts directly where everyone can be accountable. Before making any major decisions – whether to begin or end a relationship – take your time and think things through.

Mind & Spirit: Do your best to control any negative thinking at this time. You might not be using your intuition properly and may be overcome with emotion. When you heed your inner voice, you can guard against unfavorable actions or situations. There will be protection if you have the courage to embark on a new path. If you are drawn to rituals pertaining to the moon, seek guidance and research what may be drawing you toward lunar cycles. You may benefit from a reading at this time to gain insight on how best to use your spiritual gifts.

Body: Sense of smell and fight-or-flight responses are particularly affected at this time. This is also an indication that your intuition is suggesting that you get a second opinion on health matters. Beware of any substance misuse or overindulgence.

Money: Financial and professional matters may have hidden costs. Take extra care in your communication with others and ensure that you're getting the facts before making any important financial or workplace decisions. If you feel that your professionalism is under attack, have patience as things are not always what they seem. This is not the best time to make decisions that may have long-term repercussions.

Travel: A journey to clear up a misunderstanding or to visit a waterfront property.

Geography: Mediterranean, Brazil, Oceania, Chile

Locations: Oceanfront locations, cinemas, theaters, dark locations, nighttime workplaces. lakes, women's shelters, or otherwise hidden locations.

XVIII: The Moon Reversed

Overview: With Moon in reverse, you may not see things as they really are, and your judgments may be a bit off. This is not a great time to take risks because it is possible that misunderstandings and misperceptions could take place. Your intuition could also be impaired, and you might need to take time out to get realigned with our Higher Self. However, even in this position, you must be mindful of the loyalty of those around you and how they may impact your life. Take your time in processing all information to avoid any misunderstandings with others or from within.

Love: If you're waiting to hear back from a love interest, messages or responses may be delayed. If you're currently involved, this could indicate a volatile relationship. Use your intuition but your logical mind as well. Don't go off of hunches alone, put some pieces together before sitting down for a serious conversation. Not every dragon needs to be slain, so be sure to approach loved ones with respect and the intent of understanding. To ignore this advice may result in an extra heated argument.

Mind & Spirit: You may need to get helpful advice from someone who could help clear up some of your confusion or ambivalence. While this is a very intuitive time for you, it wouldn't hurt to ask for help in clearing up the many messages being received.

Body: Much like the upright position, if a diagnosis feels off in some way, ask for a second opinion and be sure to communicate all your concerns. Be careful of overindulging or substance misuse.

Money: 100 is a key figure. Misperceptions with finances and work are likely. Just when you think everything looks okay, something is off. You may be feeling extra defensive when it comes to work or money, but instead of pushing aggressively ahead, sit with your feelings and ask yourself what you might be missing. Get your facts before making any decisions or engaging in any serious talks about investment or professional issues. People around you may also not have their facts together, so it's best that you do as much research as you can on your own.

Meditations: Are you being clear in your communication or being vague to avoid confrontation? Are you allowing your emotions to cloud your judgment or responses? Are your fears preventing you from trying something new?

XIX: The Sun

Overview: The Sun card is one of creativity, joy, dreams, and accomplishment. There is something new appearing in your life. Happiness is manifesting around you, and your dreams are that much closer to becoming reality. It's time to celebrate! This is an era of accomplishment. Use past dreams and visions to manifest tangible results in the present. Opportunities present themselves and it's time to take notice and take action to make your goals happen. This is a time of new adventures, renewed health, and bright paths ahead. This is a card of fierce independence and the desire to see results after a long period of hard work. This is a time where you can accomplish what previously seemed impossible. It might also be time for a sunny vacation.

Love: This is a great time to meet new people if you're looking but remember to keep things light and take your time. This is a time where freedom and vitality are valued, so if you're single, you may be prioritizing yourself or should focus on self-care in the meantime. If you're in a committed relationship, this may be a time to evaluate what feels best about the relationship and how you can give your partner space to express their needs. This is a great card for individual freedom which is possible in any case.

Mind & Spirit: If you're looking to expand your methods of healing and self-care, this may be a great time to seek that within a community where you'll find support and meaningful ties.

Body: You may be experiencing a new burst of physical and/or creative energy. Wellness is a priority, and a positive mindset sure helps in this regard. Examine all aspects of your health where you've done well and continue to build upon great habits.

Money: Happiness may take precedence over finances and workplace priorities. This is an excellent time for business networking. If you're looking for new opportunities for employment or investment, this is an auspicious time. In any case where things go well, be sure to maintain humility and a sense of camaraderie with others. Investing in meaningful partnerships is worth far more right now even though financial prospects look good.

Travel: Migration. Making a journey of several thousand miles.

Geography: Southern Europe, Oceania

Locations: Solariums, beaches, parks, vacation destinations, maternity ward, playgrounds, daycare centers, tropical islands, or warm locations in general.

XIX: The Sun Reversed

Overview: You may need a more realistic approach to life these days. If you're looking at people or circumstances with rose-colored lenses, you may need a bit of a reality check. Things are not what they seem, and plans may not unfold the way you expect. You may be taking on more than you can handle and experience feeling overwhelmed. Be sure to acknowledge everything you should be thankful for and honor the presence of supportive loved ones in your life.

Love: Be careful not to overwhelm your partner or potential partners with dramatic displays or take their presence for granted. Complacency can kill romance, and it may be time to ensure everyone is happy – including you. Whether single or committed, maintain a bright, optimistic outlook and others may follow suit. Your self-worth matters and be sure to take that into account in or out of relationships. Be present in all that you do, especially when it comes to matters of the heart.

Mind & Spirit: You may feel somewhat imbalanced in your spiritual life or when dealing with mental health. If you're feeling stuck or unsure of how to proceed, don't hesitate to ask for help. Seek out a mentor or counselor to help answer your questions and to help you see your signposts on your journey.

Body: It may be time to adjust eating habits and ensure we are putting our wellness first. Sugar intake or levels may be out of balance. You may also want to consider taking a break or vacation to rejuvenate your body and mind. Keep a positive outlook, maintain your sense of gratitude, and things will turn out fine.

Money: 50 or 60 are important figures. If you're looking for new opportunities, be sure you don't come across as arrogant or entitled. Partnerships and networking are still key even when the Sun is in reverse, so be sure to not completely center your wants and needs. This is not a time to take anyone or anything for granted, and if you express your gratitude, wonderful opportunities may arise.

Meditations: Are you expressing gratitude for all that you have? Are you taking time to enjoy the simple pleasures of life? Are you monitoring your sugar intake? Do you feel like your freedom is being restricted?

XX: Judgment

Overview: While Judgment appears to be a card about decisions, it's also about exploring new depths of your creativity. It is ruled by Pluto and indicates a powerful transformation or rebirth. You may find that instead of jumping to conclusions, that it may be time to channel your creative mind for problem-solving. This is a period of accessing greater spiritual power and being more intentional on your spiritual journey. This is a time to trust your own perceptions, elevate your voice, and let your intentions be known.

Love: This is not a time to render harsh judgment against people you love. Instead of making assumptions, get creative about resolving conflicts. If you find that someone is repeatedly violating your boundaries, let your voice be heard to reinforce your self-respect. You can't control how people respond but you can control your own response.

Mind & Spirit: You might be surprised to find a new outlet for creative expression. This may be a spiritual path that is unexpected, or a new artistic psychosocial method used for symptom management. Keep an open mind and you may be surprised at what helps!

Body: Psychosomatic symptoms may be related to holding onto trauma. Seek out professional guidance as needed to resolve trauma-related symptoms that could lead to chronic illnesses.

Money: You hard work is not going unnoticed. Keep your head up and continue to do excellent work in every avenue involving business and financial endeavors. If you've been complacent, it's time to pick up the pace, because others are likely to judge you. Ensure you're not breaking any rules or laws in financial or workplace decisions. While this is a good time for incoming money, it's also a time to act with the utmost integrity.

Travel: You may find the ocean or sea to be of great inspiration. Plan your travels around broadening your horizons, getting out of your comfort zone, and embracing your creative side.

Geography: Oceania

Locations: Spiritual sites, rehabilitation centers, retreat sites.

XX: Judgment Reversed

Overview: When Judgment is in reverse, you might be feeling you've lost the magic touch with your creative endeavors. If you find yourself stuck in a rut or feeling indecisive, it may be time to find an outlet to express frustration – whether it's therapy or taking up a new fitness regimen. Don't bottle things up or swim in a sea of assumptions. Let your voice be heard and express how you feel!

Love: Things around you are changing and it's best to be clear about your wants, needs, and boundaries. This is not a time to become complacent, but to be proactive in telling people how you feel in real time. Don't wait for you destiny, make it happen.

Mind & Spirit: If you feel like you're getting carried away in fantasy and illusion, it may be time to investigate different grounding exercises and ways to become more present in everyday life. You may experience some sort of emotional repression, and it's best to find a means to express how you feel whether in verbal or physical form.

Body: It's time to let go of past trauma as it has already done its damage. Seek the appropriate support and guidance. Be decisive on your path to wellness.

Money: Changes are heading your way in terms of finances and professional endeavors. Put your skills to use, remain flexible, and you're likely to see a positive outcome. This is a matter of effort on your part and how much you're willing to invest in your own personal and professional excellence. If you become complacent, someone else will decide your fate for you.

Meditations: Are you properly channeling your energies in creative ways? Are you using effective problem-solving skills or becoming complacent? What's preventing you from expressing yourself? Are you speaking with your authentic voice or parroting others to save time and effort?

XXI: The World

Overview: With the World card, you can expect new opportunities to arrive within a month's time or by the next start to the lunar cycle. You may feel the weight of responsibility right now as cycles come to a close and a new chapter opens. Change can be scary, but it's certain. However, no one is an island. Reach out for help as needed and you'll realize how much you've been doing on your own. You're close to reaching a goal so don't give up! Reward yourself in the end with a well-deserved vacation or something you've always wanted.

Love: You may meet a new love interest abroad or find ways to deepen a current relationship. Think outside of the box for ways to meet new people or get creative in spicing up existing relationships. A vacation abroad may help bring a needed romantic boost.

Mind & Spirit: This is a time where you might experience a sensual awakening. You feel your intuition is heightened while exploring ways to make changes to your daily living. You may also experience an influx of prophetic or symbolic dreams. Take note of these dreams as they may be important to ideas later.

Body: An awakening of physical and holistic wellbeing. Explore different methods in which you can improve your overall health as well as your mindset.

Money: 28 and 13 are important figures. You may be experiencing overworking and not getting compensated for it to your liking. Be sure to speak up about your accomplishments and be proud of all that you've done to date. You may also find new opportunities internationally, so don't be afraid to look outside of your comfort zones for chances to elevate your career or finances.

Travel: Air travel toward a new opportunity or a new chapter in life.

Geography: Antarctica

Locations: Airports, travel hubs, or helipads.

XXI: The World Reversed

Overview: The World in reverse is a sign not to act too hastily or aggressively. Rather, trust the natural flow of things and be flexible with coming changes. Try not to upset the natural balance around you. If you find yourself trying to do too much at once, slow down and ask for help as needed. If you're feeling stuck, it may have more to do with trying to do too much on your own. You're near the end of a project or almost reaching your goal. If you're experiencing a setback, it's time for reflection.

Love: If you feel like your love life is in a bit of a rut, it may be time to think creatively about how to progress into a new chapter – whether your attached or single. Now is the time to be authentic in your romantic conversations. When you are vulnerable and share your true self, the rewards are everlasting.

Mind & Spirit: This is a time to reflect on your progress and acknowledge the abundance that already exists in your life.

Body: You may be inclined to investigate holistic or nontraditional medicine. Consult a medical professional before taking on something new but bear in mind that your mental wellness matters, too. Don't be afraid to explore your options for optimal health.

Money: When the World is in reverse, it's a time to evaluate your progress and long-term goals. Don't take opportunities for granted and don't allow others to exploit your talents. You deserve compensation for your hard work and may benefit from a mentor or adviser at this time. If you've been stuck in a financial or professional rut, you might find opportunities for growth and advancement are available if you can get out of your own way.

Meditations: Are you investing the right amount of energy into your goals? Do you fear change or are you remaining flexible for upcoming opportunities? Are you acknowledging your progress and needs?

MINOR ARCANA

In this section, you will understand the supporting structure of the tarot: the Minor Arcana. The Minor Arcana speaks of the more intimate details of our lives, whereas the Major Arcana cards refer to more prominent archetypes. The Minor Arcana consists of four suits, each associated with one of the four elements and a different layer of reality: Wands (fire) refer to the spirit, creativity, and sexuality; Cups (water) deal with the heart, emotions, and relationships; Swords (air) relate to the mind, thought, and suffering; and Pentacles (earth), with the material body, finances, and life structures.

Each of the suits contains numbered cards from Ace to Ten. These are the pips that show an evolution of the suits' spirit. Each suit also has four court cards: Pages, Knights, Queens, and Kings. Those are the personalities of the tarot, referring to stages of growth and embodiment. We will explore them all as we consider upright and reversed positions, definitions, and practical interpretations for each. The examples and meanings in this chapter will give you the keys to understanding each Minor Arcana card, which can then be used in developing a tarot language and understanding that is your own.

CUPS

Ace Of Cups

Overview: Ace of Cups indicates that there will be new love, happiness, and good health. It is an auspicious omen for new beginnings and that people will have good intentions for you in general. This is a great time to get out in socialize, meet new people, and make lasting connections. This card is about manifesting wonderful new possibilities especially in the realm of romance. This is about moving from one stage of life to the next. It is a time of emergence where you will gain greater spiritual insight in addition to an elevation in our intuition. This is also a time of great creativity, fertility, and new beginnings in love. This is a time to savor all that is sweet in life. Overall, this is quite a positive sign. Ace of Cups indicates that a wonderful new opportunity is about to take place in spiritual and physical form. Focus on positive relationships that are compatible to your lifelong journey to your Higher Self.

Love: This is a wonderful time to start new, rewarding relationships or to renew current ones with a newfound joy. If you're single, this is the perfect time to meet someone one and follow through on a commitment. If you're already attached this is an indicator that your relationship is about to move to a higher level of connection and intimacy.

Mind & Spirit: The appearance of the Ace of Cups when it comes to mind and spirit has to do with gratitude. This is an indicator that life has given you ample opportunities to receive abundance, and that it is time to pay it forward to others around you. There is an overall increase in intuition, and you may notice a heightened spiritual presence in your general environment.

Body: Your physical health should be looking good or improving very soon. Be sure that you are including colorful fruits and veggies in your daily nutrients. This is also a sign that your energy will be abundant and that your motivation will be renewed.

Money: If you're looking out for new opportunities the Ace of Cups indicates that happy new prospects await you. You're likely to find opportunities and activities where your work will be highly valued and appreciated amongst superiors and peers. If you're looking for work this indicates that the opportunities are close by, and all you have to do is say yes. When it comes to finances in general, this is a great sign. Keep an eye out for new opportunities of investment or for new business ventures.

Travel: You may take a journey after experiencing a great transformation, one in which you will greatly enjoy yourself.

Geography: North Africa, Hawaii, Jamaica, Scandinavia, North Asia, Micronesia

Locations: Lakes, ponds, or fountains.

Ace Of Cups Reversed

Overview: Ace of Cups in reverse is still a positive sign. However, you might be feeling that you're going nowhere fast. Do your best to be patient and look around you to see what might be blocking your energy. You can soon act when you examine your environment and figure out what might be standing in your way. In about 2 weeks' time, or maybe 2 months, you're likely to see some shifts.

Love: This is a sign that you might need to reevaluate your relationship or a current connection. This is not cause for alarm, but your love life might not be where you want it to be. Take a step back and figure out what it is that you really want. Seek professional guidance as needed.

Mind & Spirit: Even in the reverse position, this is still a positive card. However, you may need to take time to attend to self-care in self compassion. Do your best to meditate, seek balance, and remain grounded in your pursuit.

Body: When it comes to your health you might be doing quite well but may need to work a bit harder at self-care and making time for time for mental wellness.

Money: You may be unhappy at work or with your finances at this time due to emotional attachments. This is a time where you might want to consider transformation for the better.

Meditations: Are you trying to ignore calls for change or refusing opportunities when they arise? Are you feeling a lack of motivation? Do you need to try something new to rediscover a sense of joy? Are you letting your emotions get the best of you and trying to do too much too soon?

2 Of Cups

Overview: The Two of Cups is a card of weaving deep relationships, balance in partnerships, and things going quite well. This is a sign that something new is being spun in a current or upcoming relationship where new deeper levels of intimacy are achieved. This is a time of success in personal and professional endeavors where collaboration is highlighted. Creativity, networking, and ideas are flourishing at this time. Two of Cups indicates a potential new romance. This may also indicate a karmic connection, but it doesn't necessarily need to be romantic. This partnership, whether platonic or romantic, has great potential to be harmonious.

Love: This card represents a balance in your relationships and overall harmony when it comes to give and take. This is an auspicious omen that a genuine love relationship is occurring or about to start. While things are looking good, this is also not a time to become complacent. Nurture your relationships and seek balance in all interpersonal interactions.

Mind & Spirit: There is an increased awareness in overall emotional intelligence. You may want to seek out mental health or spiritual health routines that involve groups of people where you can exchange ideas and collaborate. This is a wonderful time to focus on your heart chakra and sharing joy with others.

Body: When it comes to your health it's highly advisable to seek out medical practitioners with whom you have great rapport. This is a positive indicator of good health and much of that will be associated with the positive mindset.

Money: 1000 is a key figure. If you're employed at the moment, it is likely that you are quite satisfied with where you are, even if it's not ideal. If you're on the lookout for new opportunities, keep your eyes open, because quite a few will be on the horizon. When it comes to income and earning potential you might be achieving balance at the moment. However, you might want to consider opportunities that might involve working close with someone to improve your situation.

Travel: You're likely to take a journey with one or more people to collaborate on a project or to enjoy a vacation for two.

Geography: Caribbean, Asia, South America, East Africa, Western Europe, South Asia, Afghanistan, Mexico, Polynesia

Locations: Networking locations or video chats for collaboration.

2 Of Cups Reversed

Overview: Two of Cups and reverse may indicate that you should be getting a handle on your fears and be more direct in addressing them. This is an indication that you might need to balance grace and gentleness with strength. This might also be an indication that you could be neglecting friendships in favor of giving too much attention to romantic ones. Seek balance in all matters of the heart. Two of cups in reverse indicates having potential disagreements with your partner or someone who you might be connected to soon. There may be a lack of balance in this partnership or relationship.

Love: If you're not being proactive in your relationships this is a time to be assertive. Remember that complacency can kill romance and there seems to be a loss of balance in a current relationship, or it may be implying that someone around you is being a bit too much of a perfectionist. If you're harboring any resentment toward someone that you care about, this is a time to lay all the cards down on the table, and perhaps think about starting over with a clean slate.

Mind & Spirit: Beware of trying to demand ultimatums or being too rigid in matters of the mind and spirit. This is a time to get centered with your heart chakra and pay attention to what you need right now to be aligned with your Higher Self.

Body: When it comes to matters of health, you might be refusing assistance from the outside. No one is an island, do not be afraid to reach out for help when you need it.

Money: You might be experiencing a sense of dissatisfaction with your work and/or finances. Take a step back and think about your priorities and where you can better collaborate with others to achieve your goals.

Meditations: Is your pride getting in the way of progress? Are you not seeing your partnerships or relationships as they really are? Are you working in a way that is unbalanced and/or alienating people?

3 Of Cups

Overview: The Three of Cups indicates fertility, happiness, and achievement. This is a time of great celebration. Healing is also highlighted as a central theme. This is a time to tap into your creativity when it comes to romance, finances, spirituality, and of course, the arts. There is much success to be had and new births, whether metaphorical or literal, are highlighted here. This card also indicates a potential reunion. If you've been far apart from someone you care about this is an auspicious omen that you are about to see one another again. Such reunions might come in the form of vacations, celebrations, weddings, or other happy occasions where many people are getting together. Three of Cups indicates a celebrating something wonderful with people you love. This is the time to enjoy all that you're grateful for with positive people in your life. This is about experiencing true joy and abundance. 3 or 3,000 are key numbers.

Love: You may be looking at a reunion with a past love. This card also indicates that if you're single a new person who is about to show up in your life might fit a lot of the criteria that you had in mind for a relationship. Look at the surrounding cards to see whether a reunion is likely or that a new person will match your ideal in in all the best ways.

Mind & Spirit: This might be an ideal time to seek out a is a spiritual or holistic consultant sent to assist you on your journey. This is not a time to go it alone. Sit with your intentions daily and think about what it is that you want and what it would take for you to be happy.

Body: This is a generally good card when it comes to physical health, but it also is a time to reflect on reflect on which areas of your health you can improve upon.

Money: 3 or 3000 ate key numbers. Money seems to be going pretty well in general even if it's causing you a bit of anxiety. Professional endeavor should be going quite well but if you're looking to make any changes be sure to be proactive about it.

Travel: You may be looking to travel westward or to a celebration.

Geography: Western United States (especially California), UK, Ireland, Scotland, New Caledonia

Locations: Bars, pubs, parties, celebrations, and weddings.

3 Of Cups Reversed

Overview: When Three of Cups appears, it is a reminder that you must not isolate too much, and that you should seek out community. Even in this position it still indicates that a reunion is likely and that you may benefit from reaching out to friends, loved ones, or family for moral support. If you've lost contact with anyone that you care about in the past few years, this might be a great time to reach out. Three of Cups in reverse indicates you might feel as though you're not truly being heard or that you're feeling misunderstood in a group of people. This might also be a time to reach out to old friends who have had your best interest at heart, but you might have lost contact.

Love: This is still a generally positive card when it comes to romance, especially if you're single. Don't be afraid to get out there and network to try to meet new people. If you're currently in a relationship you might find that financial burdens might be a main point of stress.

Mind & Spirit: You might be experiencing a resistance to change and that you may be relying too much upon the past rather than looking toward the future to create something new and exciting. Look to collaborate with others to brainstorm new ways of accomplishing your wellness and spiritual goals.

Body: You may benefit from asking others how they have improved their health over time. You may be feeling as though you could benefit from trying a new health regiment to get reenergized.

Money: When it comes to money it's important not to try to keep up with the Joneses. Be grateful for what you have and try not to get too caught up in comparing your finances or professional situation with others. You might also be dealing with workplace or professional envy. You would do well to mind your own business and not get caught up in any professional drama.

Meditations: Are you letting go of outdated modes of thinking? Are you ignoring creative opportunities? Are you not taking advantage of opportunities that are right in front of you? Are you living off of the royalties of old accomplishments instead of looking to produce new creative works? Have you stopped to give gratitude for all that you've accomplished? Are you following in pity instead of looking to find new sources of motivation?

4 Of Cups

Overview: The Four of Cups is an indicator of indicator of saudade – or a sense of melancholy of what was or what could have been. Now is not the time to bury your head in the past but to look in the present at what you can be grateful for and what you can do to advance in your life right now. Instead of wallowing and self-pity, count your blessings. Four of Cups indicates a sense of detachment or a lack of motivation. You or someone you know might be experiencing depression, especially one that is due to self-imposed circumstances. This might also indicate problems stemming from butting heads in a relationship or a love that has turned sour. Ask yourself what has brought about this sense of disappointment. Take some time to adjust your perspective and consider what you are grateful for.

Love: Right now, you might be looking at love with a sense of wistfulness. Are you thinking about someone from the past? Where do you have ideals and expectations that are excluding potential romantic partnerships that might be wonderful?

Mind & Spirit: Sometimes if you remain still and go within, not for self-pity, but for meaningful introspection, you can find the answers that you're looking for. Sometimes when you're caught up examining the past and aching for what was, you might be missing what's right in front of your face. Now is the time to sit in stillness and pay attention to small motions and opportunities that might have previously been camouflaged.

Body: This is the time to look at overall wellness from mental health to physiological health. This is not a time to become complacent about your health and it would be beneficial for you to reach out to a professional to guide you on your wellness journey.

Money: Do not despair. This is a time to go within and consider what you really want professionally or in personal finances. If you prepare quietly and thoroughly plan what you want to accomplish you will find success. This is a great time to focus on all that you have going for you instead of instead of focusing on lack.

Travel: This would be an ideal time to travel to gain perspective on what it is that you really want.

Geography: Western Europe, Oceania, South Asia, Spanish-speaking countries in South America, Fiji

Locations: Beneath a tree or a shaded area or places that are abundant with oak trees.

4 Of Cups Reversed

Overview: Four of Cups in reverse indicates that you are motivated to break free from stagnation. While there certainly can be strength in silence, it never hurts to reach out to others for support. You may be holding onto ideas too tightly to your chest. You may be overthinking plans and goals instead of acting upon them. Four of Cups in reverse indicates that any current or recent hardship is about to come to an end, and all that you've done will be rewarded.

Love: This is a great time to break free from romantic ideals of the past and make room for pleasant new opportunities to take a current relationship to another level or to meet new people. Instead of looking backward in the rearview mirror, look ahead and see what's down the road and you might be pleasantly surprised.

Mind & Spirit: Listen to your inner voice and ask yourself what it is that you really need. You might have recently found motivation to break free from a rut that you might have been sitting in for quite some time. This is progress! Don't be afraid to try out new methods for spiritual enlightenment and manifesting your goals. You might be considering alternative methods you might not have tried before.

Body: Four of Cups in reverse in regard to health may indicate that your appetites for extremes may be getting out of hand and that it might be time to think about nutrition and moderation.

Money: You're ready to break free from an unhappy situation when it comes to finances or your professional life. There is a newfound motivation that is kicking into higher gear this year which is leading you to reconsider what it's going to take for you to be happy and what long term success really means to you. You will have plenty of opportunities for advancement around you. However, you have to be proactive, or they will pass you by.

Meditations: Are you unhappy with your current accomplishments? Are you being too candid or open about your long-term plans? Are you being too impatient on your path to success? Are you ignoring your inner voice?

5 Of Cups

Overview: As is indicated with the visual component of the Rider-Waite-Smith tarot card, this is not a time to cry over spilled milk. This is a time to reassess what's important, your priorities, and what deserves your focus. You might be examining the past which covers old ground and in doing so, you might be reflecting upon your present conditions. This is the time to think about all that you have overcome and experienced and processing any remnant trauma that is impeding your growth. This is a time to determine what no longer serves you and cutting ties or cords that are holding you back. In times of despair, it can be tempting to self-isolate, but it's important to take stock of the situation as objectively as possible before making rash decisions. Any difficulties occurring now will serve as seeds of growth for future success. Five of Cups indicates a potential loss or despair. This can also indicate a mindset that focuses too much on lack. Instead of thinking about everything that you don't have, be grateful for what you do have right now.

Love: This is an indication to give yourself time and space to process any painful moments you might be experiencing relating to your romantic life. As the saying goes, things do happen for a reason. And with all endings there are new beginnings. It might be difficult to see the forest for the trees right now but know that in time things will work out for the better.

Mind & Spirit: You might be harboring resentment that is causing you more distress than you might want to admit. There is great power in forgiveness and letting go. It doesn't matter whether or not the person deserves it, the forgiveness is for yourself and to move on. It's important to release anger or any negative energies in order to be fully open to positive new beginnings.

Body: Trauma may be holding you back from living a healthy life to your fullest. If you feel that stress may be affecting your physical health this may be an ideal time to speak with someone about it.

Money: 13, 1300, 13000, or 7 million are important figures. You may be experiencing setbacks when it comes to your finances or your professional life. Do your best to remain proactive and motivated in the process. Instead of trying to force things to happen, try to go with the flow and be open to manifesting what it is that you truly want.

Travel: Travels may be related to revisiting your hometown or places where traumas have previously occurred and affected you.

Geography: Central Asia, East Africa, Western Europe, Northeast United States, South Asia, Vanuatu, Papua New Guinea, Solomon Islands

Locations: Hometowns, previous places of residence, or places related to traumatic events.

5 Of Cups Reversed

Overview: Five of Cups in reverse can indicate how the past can influence the present and the future. Unless you acknowledge and recognize the past for what it is, you're likely to repeat mistakes. This is a time to do your best to learn from past mistakes. It's important to summon up the courage to see things clearly, thoroughly, and objectively no matter how difficult it can be to face reality. This is a reminder that growth and new possibilities are right ahead of you. Five of Cups in reverse indicates that you are ready to walk away from past traumas and issues that have been holding you back. Treating all previous or current obstacles as learning lessons will help you accept a new chapter ahead.

Love: There may be disbelief or lack of faith in love or romance. This is a period where you might be feeling that your family or loved ones are causing emotional drain. An imbalance in emotions is making way for a fear of the future with little trust in romantic relationships. This could also be an indicator of divorce, separation, or general frustration in romance. The bright side of this position is that you're getting past a difficult time and recovery is possible. Keep going and don't give up. Believe in yourself.

Mind & Spirit: This might be an ideal time to interact with other people who have been on similar difficult journeys and learn how they've used different methods or techniques to process trauma and continue a healthy path to wellness. Remember that going through trauma is not something that's recommended to do alone, and it's important to acknowledge that no one is an island.

Body: In this position Five of Cups in reverse indicates that trauma might be impacting your physiological health. It's highly suggested to seek out a professional with whom you can discuss both your mental health needs and your physiological needs and coming up with an effective treatment plan for wellness and symptom management.

Money: When it comes to your professional life you may not have been feeling the most satisfied. However, it's important to point out that you have more power over your situation than you realize. It's important to remain positive and think about what it is that you really want. When it comes to finances in general, this card indicates that gratitude needs to be incorporated in your overall professional and financial outlook. This is a time to not just evaluate your pocketbook but not to base your self-esteem on your bank account.

Meditations: Are you ignoring past mistakes and how it's impacting the present? Are you not examining things carefully and objectively? Are you not digesting or processing information while it's occurring? Do you need to breathe new life into your everyday activities? Are you afraid of new beginnings? Are you letting circumstances or people intimidate you and prevent you from moving forward on your path?

6 Of Cups

Overview: When it comes to the Six of Cups, there is a possibility that a gift or opportunity is heading your way along with surprises that will tug at your heart strings. Your energy is undergoing a profound change. You may be looking forward to receiving invitations, offers, or proposals (romantic or platonic) and they may be unexpected. This is a card that indicates a renewed sense of happiness along with newfound joys in everyday life. Past ties may return to provide perspective and to deliver important new messages. There is a strong sense of nostalgia, which can serve as a source of joy, but do not become so tied to the past that you ignore the present and the future. Six of Cups indicates that you might have been feeling overwhelmed or overburdened in everyday life. This is a time to take a fun trip somewhere to reconnect with your Higher Self and recharge.

Love: When it comes to romance the Six of Cups could be an indicator that you might be looking backwards instead of in the present and toward the future. If you're currently in a relationship this may be an indicator to try new things to spice things up. If you're single, this might mean that it's time to let go of past resentments and expectations to make way for new opportunities in love. Don't allow the past to clutter up a potentially beautiful future. This card also may mean the return of an old flame but take a moment to consider if this is a viable possibility or if they need to remain in your past. This card is generally a positive omen when it comes to looking for new love, marriage, or happy emotional affairs in general.

Mind & Spirit: Six of Cups indicates that something about your energy has changed. You might find that you are receiving invitations, proposals, offers, and other messages that you didn't expect, and they will be coming rapidly. At this time, you might be experiencing lucid or prophetic dreams and reminiscing on past life experiences. You can start to see people in situations from your past and how they've had positive effects on what we're doing in the present. This is a period of renewed happiness and making peace with the past.

Body: This card indicates that any health problems you might be experiencing at the moment may be connected to childhood or genetic conditions stemming from hereditary sources. It might be important to reach out to a therapist to talk through any residual childhood trauma. You might also want to reach out to family members to get a clearer picture of your family's medical history.

Money: When it comes to professional and financial opportunities this is a great time to flex your creative muscles. Any business or professional ventures having to do with the arts are likely to be quite promising. Even if it's just a hobby or something that you do in your spare time, this is a great time to invest in your artistic side. If you're looking for extra money or ways to invest, look for signs and signals that are reminiscent of childhood or retro themes.

Travel: You may be taking a journey to a place where you might be tempted by someone from your past.

Geography: West Africa, Chile, Vanuatu, Australia, South Asia

Locations: Hotel bars, retro art exhibits, reunions, or flower shops.

6 Of Cups Reversed

Overview: Six of Cups in reverse indicates a lack of decision making that is causing emotional distress. This also denotes that anything that you might have been planning or set in motion might experience a delay. It doesn't mean that things won't work out, it just means that it may take longer than expected. This also indicates that you might be living in the past and/or allowing the past two prevent you from moving forward. If you refuse to progress past old issues and people, you might be finding yourself rehashing the same old dramas over and over again. It's time to move on or the present will never change. Six of Cups in reverse indicates that you might be holding on to the past too tightly. This is a time to loosen your grip on everything behind you if you want to see happiness and success ahead.

Love: There may be indecision when it comes to romance or marriage. It also indicates that there may be someone behaving irresponsibly in a current relationship. If you're dealing with a separation or divorce, it's time to look within define personal growth, empowerment, and happiness. Six up Cups in reverse also indicates that there may be a relationship that has been beneficial in the past but might no longer be suitable for you in the present or the future. Remember, you must be proactive about your love life and if you're looking for new romance or to improve the current relationship, you have to be an active participant.

Mind & Spirit: When it comes to your own personal growth, it's important to be accountable for the part you play in your own misery. This is not about placing blame but seeing how you might have allowed certain circumstances to exist. As the saying goes, what you tolerate you validate. You might not be able to control the behavior of others, but you can control how you respond and decide whether or not something needs to persist in your life. You have more power in your situation then you might realize.

Body: This indicates that you might not be completely mindful when it comes to your physiological health. If you don't take time for your wellness, you'll need to take time off to attend your illness.

Money: You might be reaching a point in your professional life where you're no longer satisfied or challenged by your everyday routine. This is not a time to despair but to start planning ahead for the future. Not every dragon needs to be slain, sometimes it can be befriended. Do your best to look objectively at your finances and or professional life and ask yourself if what you're doing right now is worth it or beneficial for your long-term. If you find that certain circumstances have gone way past their shelf life, this is a time to be proactive about planning for your future. The choice is up to you.

Meditations: Are you allowing nostalgia to trip you up in the present and prevent you from planning for a happier future? Are you trying to rush your personal development? Are you locked into outdated thinking patterns? Are you refusing to leave your rut because it's become your comfort zone?

7 Of Cups

Overview: The Seven of Cups indicates that this is a time to make necessary decisions if you're looking to meet your goals. This is a confirmation that you are on the right track, and you should pursue your goals. When this card appears, any decision that you make will be followed up within a very short time – typically within two weeks with the confirmation that the decision you've made was the correct one. If your decision is incorrect, you will find out soon enough followed by opportunities to get yourself out of an undesirable situation. This may indicate that some hard work is up ahead, but the following results will be impactful. This is especially important time to protect your plans and not share what you're doing with others. You may want to consider shielding your energy and protecting yourself as well as your intentions from external influences. Seven of Cups indicates coming to a decision after examining a variety of options. Be objective, weigh the pros and cons, and face the music.

Love: You might be facing several choices when it comes to your romantic life and options. Take the time to consider what it is that you truly want in a relationship – if at all – and be sure to be honest with yourself and others about your intentions. This is not a time to force anything to happen in current or potential relationships, but it is a signal not to accept the status quo either. If your love life needs work, there's no need to be aggressive or give ultimatums. Go with the flow and be real about your needs and what you bring to the table.

Mind & Spirit: This is an important time to sit down and get to focusing and writing your affirmations. If you have some written, be sure to revisit them daily and to adjust them as you accomplish your goals. Life is a marathon, not a sprint. Start a vision board, a creative bullet journal, or any helpful tool to help you manifest your dreams on the path to your Higher Self.

Body: This is an important time to get back on track with your health and finding a sense of balance in mind and body. Be sure to document any new symptoms or ailments in a daily journal if in the event you need to consult a healthcare provider.

Money: Any professional opportunities or investments must be carefully examined before moving forward. Trust your senses right now. If the energy doesn't feel right, then you're probably right. Anything having to do with numbers carries an extra weight of doubt. However, if you're currently working on a creative endeavor, this is an auspicious omen that all will turn out well.

Travel: You might be experiencing overwhelming feelings when it comes to travel. This is an important time to get organized and not get too flustered with making decisions.

Geography: Suriname, Australia

Locations: Jewelry stores, patisseries, or candy shops.

7 Of Cups Reversed

Overview: Seven of Cups in reverse indicates that you may need to pull back and retreat for some time. You may need to be more protective of all your plans and yourself most of all. If you're looking for a major transformation, this is an indicator that you may need to reexamine your approach in accomplishing your dreams. Seven of Cups in reverse indicates that you might be possibly avoiding a situation and spending a lot of time in your head swimming in fantasy and delusions. This is a time to get your head out of the clouds and back into reality if you want your dreams to manifest.

Love: This is a time of clarity in your romantic life. You're coming to terms with what you want and need to be happy. This is a time to trust your intuition, and don't be afraid to state your boundaries aloud. Focus less on how you'll be received and be more intentional about what you want. People who genuinely care about you will honor your boundaries and will not treat your basic needs like burdens.

Mind & Spirit: This is an ideal time for spiritual self-care. After a period of difficulty, it's important to take time to get centered with self-compassion and love. Instead of looking outside of you for the answers, take time to meditate and focus on searching for everything you seek within. Don't be afraid of being assertive in your own well-being.

Body: This is a time to be proactive about taking care of yourself – and will include consulting the appropriate healthcare providers for further insight. Don't delay in your wellness and be proactive instead of reactive.

Money: This is a time to be extra careful in trusting others around you in financial and professional endeavors. Trust your instincts when it comes to even the most benign of red flags. You may also find yourself overwhelmed when it comes to choices for investment, but just do your homework and then act.

Meditations: Do you need to reexamine how you're approaching your goals? Are you over sharing your plans with others while they are in progress? Is it time to abandon a goal so that you can focus on a better one?

8 Of Cups

Overview: The Eight of Cups indicates that you may be searching and working for a greater good. You may become more industrious when it comes to building community for others or yourself. Right now, you are very strong and capable of so much more than you realize. When this card appears, it indicates that there may be some dissatisfaction with old systems, the way things used to be, and outdated beliefs. You might also find that some things are no longer as fulfilling as they used to be. This is an especially important time to harness your power, redesign your life, and manifest your dreams through hard work. Eight of Cups represents spending time in introspection and the need to let go of outdated modes of thinking and things that no longer serve you. It may be scary to walk away, but it appears to be necessary to find genuine happiness.

Love: This is a generally good card when it comes to partnership. If you're single and looking this may indicate that you might meet someone while working toward a good cause. If you're currently in a relationship, this may be an indicator that you can improve your romantic life through doing something kind for your community with your loved one. This is a card of strength and being assertive in love and your emotions.

Mind & Spirit: Eight of Cups when it comes to mind and spirit indicates that you need to re-evaluate your own individual role in spirituality and how you want to interact with the world around you. If you're looking to expand your knowledge about spirituality, this may be a great time to think outside of the box and consider doing something that you've never done before. You may be searching for deeper spiritual meaning.

Body: When it comes to your physiological health you may be sensing that you've been putting yourself in unnecessary danger or are involved in activities that might be to your detriment. Don't ignore health concerns, listen to your body.

Money: When it comes to your professional life you may find that your efforts, no matter how persistent, may be stifled by outdated systems and ways of thinking. You see yourself coming up with new plans and ideas that improve the community or reinvent systems to serve a new purpose. If you're looking to invest this may be a great time to think about putting money toward supporting innovative new ideas that tackle outdated systems or modes of living that no longer makes sense.

Travel: If you're looking to travel anytime soon, this is an indicator that your plans should workout accordingly. Trips may involve letting go of outdated situations, working in new circumstances, and letting go of the past.

Geography: Scandinavia, Guyana, Bolivia, Australia

Locations: Thrift shops or antique dealers.

8 Of Cups Reversed

Overview: the Eight of Cups in reverse indicates that you might be in a situation or role that is no longer satisfying to you. If you have any doubts or if there are any unknown circumstances now is not the time to act. If you find that life is becoming increasingly cumbersome or unfulfilling, look around you and see if others are not following through on their promises or responsibilities. Eight of Cups in reverse indicates that you should be on guard about becoming too materialistic or fearful, which may be preventing you from moving forward.

Love: You may be turning to introspection regarding your romantic life. If you're currently involved, you may be thinking about breaking up. If you're single, this may be about walking away from current circumstances and potential romances that seem to be going nowhere. Take time to think about what you want and need, then communicate accordingly. If you still find that your needs are not being met, you can then act on the next new chapter ahead.

Mind & Spirit: This is a time to emerge from a spiritual rut and make meaningful connections with others. This is a time to have conversations and healthy interactions with others instead of self-imposed isolation. There is nothing wrong with having support on your journey.

Body: Your energies and current physical health may feel stuck somehow, which could be leading to stress manifesting in physical symptoms. You have the power to make positive changes to your health.

Money: You may be feeling dissatisfied with current professional or financial endeavors. You might be feeling as though you want to start from scratch and what you're doing is no longer cutting it. Get professional advice before making any long-lasting decisions.

Meditations: Are you looking for a quick fix or an easy way out? Are you neglecting reality and everyday duties? Are you building a solid foundation for long term success? Are you being patient with yourself or others? Are you making things more complicated than they should be? Are you violating any boundaries when it comes to your own abilities?

9 Of Cups

Overview: The Nine of Cups generally signifies that a wish is going to be fulfilled. It is a sign of luck and protection in which your wishes begin to be fulfilled in the near future. Sometimes this time span can range from nine months to a year and a half. This card indicates that a time of luck in your life is coming soon and that you may look toward autumn for big changes. This also indicates new happiness, growth, and material satisfaction. Over the next few months, you might find that luck is working out for you in achieving higher levels in work or social status. Seven is also a lucky number at this time. Nine of Cups indicates positive energy and wish fulfillment. This is a card of a dream or plan coming to fruition. Take the time now to express your gratitude for all that you've accomplished. This is a wish fulfilled and you deserve it.

Love: This is a very positive card whether you're currently in a relationship or single. You can expect interpersonal interactions to be very positive and efforts to deepen intimacy will be successful. This is also an optimal time to socialize and meet new people.

Mind & Spirit: This is an ideal time to work on your affirmations and putting those goals out into the Universe. If you don't have a vision board, this is a great time to design the life that you truly want. Don't be afraid to dream too big right now. This is the wish card, so put your wishes into visual and tangible form, and watch your dreams take flight right before your eyes.

Body: This is generally a good card when it comes to your health, and if you're undergoing any treatments or testing, you're likely to hear positive news. This is also a great time to work on daily living and exercise habits that you've been wanting to try and will keep you motivated.

Money: When it comes to finances and professional endeavors, this is an extremely auspicious omen. If you've been working on long-term plans, you can see previous delays and obstacles dissipate within a month's time. If you've been looking for new professional opportunities, you can expect to hear good news very soon. When it comes to your finances an investment, try to visualize what it means to be truly stable and happy in the long term. Are you working to build the foundations to your happiest life? If not, this is the time to not only start planning, but putting your words into action.

Travel: You're about to embark on a journey or a vacation that you've been wanting to take for quite some time. This is a dream trip that you've been thinking about for years.

Geography: South Asia, East Coastline of North America, Western Europe, East Africa, Australia

Locations: Bars, pubs, or fortune-teller sites.

9 Of Cups Reversed

Overview: The Nine of Cups in reverse indicates that someone or something is preventing your wish from being fulfilled. You may need to reestablish your boundaries with other people. Or you may be trying to push too hard too soon in fulfilling your wishes and dreams. It's important to work hard to manifest your goals but you must also allow yourself the time and space to let events unfold and manifest in a time that is right. Nine of Cups in reverse indicates that you might be feeling a bit entitled. Be careful when manifesting from a place of lack. Focus on what it is that you want and how to bring it into fruition.

Love: This is a wonderful time for deepening relationships, whether new or existing, and taking the time to cherish intimate conversations and lively social events.

Mind & Spirit: This is a time for mindful introspection and spending quality time getting connected with your Higher Self. Think about incorporating your spiritual practices into your everyday routine.

Body: You may be experiencing issues with joints, especially knees, or issues with skin discoloration. While this card is generally a positive one, it's also a signal to go deeper in terms of any present ailments or health concerns.

Money: Your professional life should be going smoothly and you're likely to find gratitude and credit for your work. If you're looking for opportunities, you're likely to find something that fits your needs quite soon. In terms of finances, try not to focus on figures but rather what makes you truly happy. However, you're also likely to see financial rewards very soon.

Meditations: Are you protecting your dreams? Are you allowing external influences to sway you from your path? Are you trying to do too much at the same time? Are you placing limitations on your goals and dreams? Are you trying to force things to happen instead of allowing things to happen in their own time?

10 Of Cups

Overview: The Ten of Cups is a card of great happiness. You might find that places exposed to the sun or are generally warm are quite lucky for you. This is a time to trust your inner voice and know that good luck and good connections are on the way to recharge your spirit and open the door for new opportunities. If you take the initiative and make a move, you will see hopes and dreams manifest before your eyes. Ten of Cups indicates achieving a sense of fulfillment especially when it comes to love and relationships. This could also indicate a relationship that holds the potential to be a lifelong romance. This is generally a positive omen for happy home life.

Love: You are likely to be in sync with those you love. If you're looking for a romantic commitment or taking a relationship to another level, be on the lookout for positive new changes.

Mind & Spirit: When it comes to your spiritual life this is an indicator that if you really want to realize your hopes and dreams you have to get out of thinking mode and act. This is not a time to rest on your laurels. If you've made promises to yourself or to someone, this is a time to follow through.

Body: Your health is likely to be generally good and you're likely to overcome any outstanding issues. Examine your overall wellness and look for areas for potential improvement and ways to cope with hereditary ailments. Try not to fret about things you cannot control and seek out guidance as needed to put your mind at ease.

Money: This is a time where your professional expertise is proving to be invaluable. It seems that your professional endeavors are going quite well but it's also a reminder not to get complacent. In terms of finances, things might be going quite well as a result of your hard work. Be sure to share the wealth of your expertise with others around you and sharing your rewards in positive and healthy ways.

Travel: Journeys are likely to be quite positive and to dreamy destinations for rest and relaxation. This may also be a trip where you are treating others and sharing in your abundance.

Geography: Asia, Australia

Locations: Sunny places and/or all-inclusive resorts.

10 Of Cups Reversed

Overview: The Ten of Cups in reverse indicates that you should stop trying to do things the way other people do them or you're going to continue to experience difficulties. You might be dealing with discouragement after not seeing progress for some time. There is a great desire to push things forward and it might be affecting your health. You might also be making yourself vulnerable to others around you who have hurt your feelings, and this might be preventing you from taking necessary action. If you're patient, you will see progress. Ten of Cups in reverse indicates feeling disconnected with others around you or possible dysfunction in one's home. Figure out ways to bring harmony into your own space.

Love: This is not a time to rely on old and outdated relationship patterns, but to look within and to trust your inner voice in terms of what you want in your romantic life. This is also not a time to be impulsive. While you should live in the moment, you should also be mindful of building toward a positive future with someone you love. This is also a warning to not stare too long in the rearview mirror when it comes to your romantic life. Do your best to be mindful and grateful in any potential or current relationships. If someone has walked out of your life, there is a reason for it. There is no sense in looking back when you have what you need right here and right now. Also, it's important to be mindful of having realistic expectations when it comes to love. This is not about being with the perfect person but about being with someone who is perfect for you.

Mind & Spirit: This is a time to be mindful of all that you have to be grateful for in life. Remember that comparison is a thief of joy. Sometimes it's possible to overlook all the wonderful blessings you have in your life and focus on the negative. Take the veil off in see what's before you.

Body: be careful of overdoing any exercise or wellness regimen. This is not a time to be overly aggressive or to try to reach standards that you're not prepared to reach. Give yourself both time and grace to accomplish your health and wellness goals. It might also be beneficial to consult with a professional in this field to have a more realistic outlook on your short-term and long-term needs.

Money: This is a good indication that you are a subject matter expert in your field, and that people are generally working well with you. If you're looking for new opportunities, you're likely to find positive prospects very soon. This is also an auspicious omen that any potential financial problems or likely to end sometime soon and new opportunities will manifest. Be sure to continue to express gratitude.

Meditations: Are you being mindful of the things that you say? Are you being too reliant on the opinions of others instead of listening to your inner voice? Are you looking before you leap? Are you afraid of making a move out of a fear of change? Are you repeating old cycles that no longer benefit you?

Page Of Cups

Overview: The Page of Cups indicates good luck and new birth. Look out for good news and new opportunities for creative inspiration. However, you must be cautious when starting any new endeavors. You must do your best to camouflage your plans as much as possible, especially while you're doing it. If you manage to do that, and keep your ongoing progress to yourself, you will open the door to wonderful new experiences that lay a solid foundation for the future ahead. Page of Cups indicates someone who is very creative and likes to talk of romance and travel. They might also be a bit childish and a bit of a dreamer. However, keep an open mind with this person as they might have answers that you didn't think of or could help you with a creative project.

Love: You might be dealing with someone who is a bit younger than you and possibly a little childish. If you're in a current or established relationship, this could indicate the need for a bit of playfulness but also not some neglect responsibilities. This is a time to not take anything or anyone too seriously, and to be both compassionate and encouraging with those we love. This person in question may also have a very youthful energy and could be quite romantic. This is not a time to engage in serious conversations but to take things lightly.

Mind & Spirit: This is a time to be mindful of getting out of a spiritual rut but to also have fun in your routines, rituals, and all that you do when it comes to spirituality. Try to take things lightly and look at things from a perspective of your younger self.

Body: You may be experiencing issues with your feet or with fussy eating habits. Exercise a bit of compassion with yourself and others when it comes to either issue. Also, consider any symptoms that are standing out and are trying to tell you something.

Money: If you've been feeling like you've been stuck in an unrewarding financial or professional position this is an auspicious omen for having new opportunities come your way. This is an indication that you have the power to make much needed changes and to be proactive about your finances.

Travel: You're likely to take leisurely travel and do your best to enjoy the simple pleasures in life.

Geography: Southern Europe, Bolivia, Spanish-Speaking countries of Central America, Northeastern US, Australia

Locations: Recreational sports venues, date night activities

Page Of Cups Reversed

Overview: Page of Cups in reverse indicates that new possibilities cannot happen unless you get rid of outdated thinking or old ways of being. This is time to shed that dead skin. There may be obstacles on your path at the moment. Maybe circumstances or people are blocking your growth. Take a look at everything and everyone around you with an objective eye. If you fail to do so you may be hindering your own progress. Page of Cups in reverse indicates someone who could potentially be immature, especially when dealing with problem-solving or conflict. There may be a situation involving this person and substance misuse or negative coping mechanisms. This might also indicate that you need to re-evaluate your plans and moving forward as they could potentially be unrealistic.

Love: Page of Cups in reverse is caution sign when it comes to romance. It's an indicator of displaced affections, and quite possibly a sense of unhappiness or rejection relating to relationships. You may be dealing with someone who is blocking your progress or taking more than they give when it comes to personal growth. This is an important time to take the rose-colored glasses off and look at situations and relationships with an objective lens, especially when someone is truly not making themselves available to you. If you fail to do this, will most likely experience additional setbacks and delays in accomplishing your goals. It's time to put up some boundaries with this person and take them off the pedestal.

Mind & Spirit: Page of Cups in reverse indicates that you might be experiencing disappointment after a long period of emotional exhaustion. You might have had high hopes for a person or for a project to work out but find yourself feeling overwhelmed and drained. You might also be neglecting your own gifts and talents, especially when it pertains to the occult. There appears to be obstacles in your path at this time that are hindering your spiritual growth.

Body: You may be experiencing issues with skin or skin care in general. You might also need to go through a phase of growth that must occur after a period of transformation in the shedding of old skin. This is not a time for quick fixes or fads.

Money: This is generally a positive card when it comes to finances or one's professional life. Just be careful to always keep yourself accountable and not to display any level of hubris with those you work with or those you're investing with. If you find yourself feeling uncertain about the future ahead, this might be a good time to seek out a trusted advisor or someone you know who could help guide the way. This is also not a time for any frivolous purchases.

Meditations: Are you trying to do way more than you need to? Are you hanging on to outdated thinking? Are you not being assertive in accomplishing your goals? Are you trying to skip ahead or look for easy ways out? Are you neglecting to ask for help or rejecting it? Are you being disciplined in getting things done?

Knight Of Cups

Overview: The Knight of Cups indicates intuitive insight and protecting yourself through the power of stillness. This is a great card when it comes to mysticism. However, it's important to camouflage yourself as there may be untrustworthy people around. This is a time to go within, be still in body and mind to receive new insight from the Universe as to what steps you should take next. Knight of Cups represents someone who is creative and calm. This is someone that you are potentially dealing with right now who might have difficulty following through. You might also be experiencing a lot of different ideas and inspirations at this time, and you might not know how to put them into action. Write some of these ideas down, even if you don't know how to proceed. This is an indication that even if you don't have the tools now to manifest your goals, they're coming soon.

Love: This is an indication that there is an intense relationship that is either about to occur or is happening in real time. There may be relationships or romantic ties when it comes to karmic cycles and partners. There is a possibility that someone is absorbing another person's individuality or personality to create a new sense of self. Remember that when it comes to love it's not about losing yourself but ripening into a better person together.

Mind & Spirit: To enhance creativity and healing it's important to sit quietly in meditation. Sometimes when you go within and exercise mindful introspection, you can awaken dormant abilities and then manifest your own dreams through the power of intuition while protecting yourself accordingly. Be open to messages from your spirit guides and know that any coincidences happening around you are for a reason.

Body: This is an important time to make time for wellness. While this is still a positive card it may be time to consider whether or not you are pushing yourself too hard. Take it easy.

Money: Professional endeavors are likely to manifest with positive, tangible results. This is a time to reflect on all that you've accomplished throughout your professional career. If you're looking to improve your financial situation, this is a generally good omen.

Travel: You might be receiving an invitation to an upcoming celebration. Whether it's a reunion, a party in general, or a wedding. You might be seeing a loved one or a family member quite soon. You may also be making travel plans with a new friend or love interest.

Geography: Kenya, China, New Zealand

Locations: Romantic terraces, waterfront dinner locations, buildings with panoramic views, or bridges.

Knight Of Cups Reversed

Overview: Knight of Cups in reverse indicates that you might need to examine what others around you are doing and what you're doing to accomplish your goals. This is an indication that there is too much force in trying to accomplish goals. Your activities may result in you or others getting injured if you are too complacent. Wherever you are, exercise caution and situational awareness. Trust may be broken so take care to do everything you can to be aware of people and situations especially when it comes to potential dangers and safety risks. Others around you may have good intentions but you might not be able to rely on them. There may be hidden dangers lurking in the shadows. Exercise caution. Knight of Cups in reverse indicates someone who might like to jump to conclusions and overreact. This may also indicate a relationship that has lost its spark.

Love: If you're looking to send a message to someone you love or care about, there might be delays in reception. Knight of Cups in reverse indicates someone who is potentially being an emotional drain or causing a loss or separation. Take extra care in trusting people around you, especially those who have a history of dishonesty or procrastinating when it comes to meeting your needs. This also speaks of a person who might have been quite charming at first, saying and doing all the right things. However, behavior might have changed to a more complacent and passive attitude. This is going from a whirlwind relationship to something duller and unfulfilling. You might also find that this person leaves you feeling quite overwhelmed.

Mind & Spirit: This might be a difficult time to focus on your spiritual life. You might not have the time that you want or need to get to your spiritual goals. However, doing something small counts and can be quite effective over the long-term.

Body: Try not to take too many drastic measures when it comes to your health and fitness regimen. Do your best to maintain a positive state of mindfulness. Try not to go to any extremes when it comes to exercise at this time.

Money: When it comes to your professional life, you might find yourself feeling a bit burned out. This is quite possibly a time to start planning for a relaxing getaway. When it comes to finances, you might find yourself worrying about your short-term future a bit more lately. It's important to maintain a positive mindset and know that this is possibly a time to sit back and reflect on what you really want.

Meditations: Are you letting others know your plans before they manifest? Are others around you being secretive? Are you being patient? Do you need time to go within an meditate to clear your mind? Are you missing out on wonderful opportunities because you're trying to push too hard on certain goals? Are people around you being truthful?

Queen Of Cups

Overview: The Queen of Cups indicates a heightened intuition and spiritual empowerment. This may be a good time to focus on your spirituality especially at night. You might have been feeling perceptive in dark times, and you might be finding yourself tapping into your own intuition and that it's been more accurate than ever. Dreams are likely to become true and you may be finding that clairvoyant abilities are helping you connect dreams with reality. This heightened sensitivity is a good thing. Your determination is about to pay off and be rewarded. Look forward to new success and pleasures ahead. Queen of Cups indicates someone who is very intuitive and receives messages from their Higher Self. This is a loving person who possesses the energy to help manifest wonderful things in a time that you need it most. This is a very nurturing person who could help you out in a time of need.

Love: The Queen of Cups, is a positive omen when it comes to a current relationship. If you're a single at this time, this indicates that you're likely to find a positive new relationship quite soon. However, it's also important to look at love with a realistic lens. It's okay to be excited but try to remain grounded about your expectations.

Mind & Spirit: You might find that your intuitive abilities are especially heightened at this time. Someone in your life., especially with an abundance of feminine energy, may provide additional insight to help you get in touch with your Higher Self and channel. Important spiritual messages.

Body: This is a time to be compassionate with yourself, especially when it comes to physical wellness. If you're holding onto trauma or anything else causing you grief, this is a great time to release that and let it go. Sometimes when you hold onto negative thought patterns and memories, they can have an additional negative impact on your health. Do your best to think positively and to align your goals and values with your Higher Self.

Money: When it comes to any professional endeavors, this is an indication that you might receive help or assistance that is highlighted with precision and intuition. When it comes to matters of personal finance, this is a great sign that you will have your needs met in terms of financial prosperity. Also think of ways that are creative when it comes to making money. This is also a great indication to invest in women-led organizations.

Travel: This is an excellent time to plan a trip where you can get more in touch with your Higher Self or a place where you feel most connected to Source.

Geography: Europe, New Zealand

Locations: Art classes, beachfront locations, spa, or a healer's office.

Queen Of Cups Reversed

Overview: Queen of Cups in reverse indicates that you might not be staying balanced or grounded when it comes to exploring your own psychic abilities and intuitive gifts. Your belief system may need a checkup. If you're someone who is working in the field of mediums or anything pertaining to the metaphysical you might need to practice grounding meditations and exercises. This is a time to also shed old beliefs. Queen of Cups in reverse indicates you or someone you know that could be weighed down by their emotions. This is not a time to suppress how you feel and if you do not speak with your authentic voice, you can find yourself feeling disconnected from your Higher Self.

Love: You might be involved in a relationship that is spiritually draining and you might feel that you've been deceived. If you're single, be extra careful in placing your trust in the hands of people who might not have earned it. If you're sensing any inauthenticity in romance, take it as a red flag. This is a time to treat yourself and others around you with love and compassion, but to also set clear boundaries – especially with those who have demonstrable anger issues or a recent and drastic behavioral change.

Mind & Spirit: This is an indicator that the energies of others around you may be overstimulating or overexaggerated and affecting you as a result. This is not a time to give into illusions or embellishments. Your perception or the perception of others may lack depth, and someone may be trying to trick you into believing something that is not true or withholding valuable information.

Body: This is an important time to be extra compassionate with yourself as it pertains to physical health and healing unresolved drama. No matter how you might compartmentalize it, remember that your body keeps the score. Longstanding resentments may be causing significant health problems if left unattended.

Money: In your professional life, you might be experiencing someone who is being. Unreasonable or generally difficult to deal with. Be wary of anyone who is exhibiting overly controlling behaviors or faulty judgment. Try to remember that you attract more flies with honey than with vinegar. This is a time to exercise diplomacy and not be too aggressive. If you're looking to invest money, this is a time to be extra cautious and not gamble with any money that you can't do without.

Meditations: Are you seeing things for as they are or how you want them to be? Are you ignoring your inner voice? Is it time to get rid of outdated beliefs?

King Of Cups

Overview: The King of Cups is about trusting in the power of love and light. At this time, you may be perceiving the most subtle movements, and your intuition may be heightened. This is a time to come forward in sharing what you've been working on within the past year or so. Remember you are made of love and light. This is a time to express your creative energies. This is a time of transformation and emotional maturity. Look to your visions and see that loving light reflected in everything that you do and how it pertains to healing creativity and compassion for others. Your skill set will soon be acknowledged by others, and you will be sought out for your advice. King of Cups indicates you or someone who is graceful and compassionate. This may also indicate that you should take time to reflect upon your current circumstances, especially if anything is triggering troublesome or traumatic memories.

Love: King of Cups indicates someone who is emotionally mature, family-oriented, and very loving. This is a person who is long-term relationship material – if not marriage material. If you're single, you can anticipate someone who matches this description is likely to come along and will suit your expectations. This is a sign of a mature romantic partner who is loving, kind, and supportive. When you set your boundaries, the right person will respect them and you.

Mind & Spirit: The Universe is conspiring to work with you. This is an important time to maintain balance between masculine and feminine energies. Take time to meditate on what it is that you truly need and plan to act accordingly. Explore different meditation styles or sources of inspiration that can help you be more proactive.

Body: This is a time to trust in the medical advice of professionals and to give yourself time to heal. This is generally a positive omen when it comes to anticipating any news pertaining to physical health. Make sure that you're taking enough time for self-care. And practicing a healthy fitness and wellness regimen while being mindful of nutritional intake.

Money: If you're looking to invest, this might be a good time to consider real estate or anything having to do with the visual or culinary arts. You might also be looking to expand your professional and financial horizons by going overseas or focusing your interest on investing near a coastal city.

Travel: You can expect travel plans to take place, ideally near a body of water or an island where self-care will be of the most importance.

Geography: Japan, Russia, New Zealand

Locations: Psychotherapy offices, riverfront locations, or an elderly relative's home.

King Of Cups Reversed

Overview: King of Cups in reverse indicates that you might not be seeing things quite clearly. Perhaps you need to reexamine your own perception of a situation or person. Someone might try to mislead you. This is an important time to seek balance in your emotions or work on emotional maturity.

Love: King of Cups in reverse indicates the presence of an emotional vampire. You might find yourself being manipulated by someone who is potentially trying to emotionally blackmail you. This is an important time to reflect upon your close relationships and ask yourself if this person should still be on your journey with you. Be careful in throwing caution to the wind and making risky, romantic decisions. This is an important time to balance emotion with logic.

Mind & Spirit: King of Cups in reverse indicates that you need to proceed with caution with anything pertaining to your spiritual development. This is not a time to take shortcuts when it comes to your spiritual life, accessing your intuition, or getting in touch with your Higher Self. It's not enough to just follow up or go along with the crowd when it comes to spiritual matters. Take time to think things through before committing to any new ritual or spiritual path. Be careful of following the advice of superficial gurus or people cosplaying the spirituality of cultures other than their own.

Body: This is an important time to simply follow medical advice and to focus on self-care. This is still quite a positive card regarding health and any upcoming news. However, take care not to give into any fads regarding diet or health in general. If a solution seems too good to be true, it probably is.

Money: You might be dealing with issues with someone with hyper-masculine energy pertaining to your professional life or your finances. While unprofessional behavior should be monitored, it's important to take a step back and figure out the best way forward. You could also be dealing with someone who is throwing caution to the wind regarding finances or your professional realm. Be careful of any get rich quick schemes or taking too big of a gamble with a significant amount of money. This is a time to be practical and not to dream of overwhelming riches that come quickly.

Meditations: Are you neglecting your inner voice? Are you over analyzing the situation? Are you seeing things as they are? Are you ignoring your intuition? Are you refusing to see red flags? Are you not looking within for your own answers?

PENTACLES

Ace Of Pentacles

Overview: The Ace of Pentacles indicates a time of material prosperity and abundance. This is a time where you will find that abundance is available if you know how to access it. Abundance will not simply land on your lap, but it can arrive if you make an effort. At this time, it would be best to follow the path of least resistance, not being too assertive or aggressive but trusting in the Universe that everything will manifest in its own time. You are entering a period in which success becomes part of your ventures. A foundation has been laid and your plans should come to fruition. Ace of Pentacles indicates that manifestations could occur and that obstacles are no longer blocking your way to achieve abundance. This is the time to give energy and focus into manifesting your dreams in tangible form. Think of the law of attraction and giving positive affirmations to the Universe.

Love: Ace of Pentacles indicates a relationship or potential new partnership with financial security. If you are currently in a relationship, you may find romance and intimacy being taken to another level. If you're unattached, this is a good omen for meeting someone new through an event or networking opportunity.

Mind & Spirit: This is a time to embrace new spiritual paths that could help you remain grounded and focused. This is a great time to be spontaneous and shake things up! You may be pleasantly surprised by the rewards and outcome.

Body: Improved health conditions are highlighted so long as negative people don't cause additional and unnecessary stress. Make sure that you're examining all aspects of your physical health and doing your best to achieve balance and meet your goals, as increased focus will have great rewards. This is also an ideal time to seek out new ways to enhance your physical health.

Money: New beginnings are ahead especially pertaining to increasing long-term financial prosperity. Money may come from unexpected places at this time, or you may be receiving a bonus, inheritance, or some other financial gain that is significant and helpful. You could be starting a new job or embarking upon a promising financial endeavor. This is an ideal time to pay off debt or to simply set aside money for the future.

Travel: You may be relocating for work or to start a new chapter in your life that is rooted in security.

Geography: Northern part of the United States bordering Canada, North Africa, Hawaii, Jamaica, Scandinavia, North Asia, Micronesia, Central Africa

Locations: Banks, currency exchange centers, or stock exchange.

Ace Of Pentacles Reversed

Overview: Ace of Pentacles in reverse indicates that you might be trying to push too hard when it comes to success and material acquisition. This is a reminder not to force anything or else you're going to deal with a significant amount of discouragement, frustration, and lack. This is a time to go with the flow and find your rhythm on the path to manifestation. There may be some delays and plans may not materialize at this time. There is also the possibility that you're experiencing a false sense of security and you should be aware of overdoing anything. This is a time to exercise gratitude and not to push too hard in ambitions. Ace of Pentacles in reverse indicates a potential partnership or opportunity may be lost or that you might experience a setback in achieving a goal.

Love: Be cautious of excessive greed or materialism in romantic relationships. You may be dealing with someone who is taking more than they are giving, and is, in turn, affecting your ability to feel safe and happy. Remember, comparison is a thief of joy. If you're single, you may be meeting a potential new partner through professional networking, a conference, or through work.

Mind & Spirit: This is an ideal time to reach out to a community or others who are on a similar spiritual path for camaraderie or guidance. It's important to expand your spiritual horizons and to not be afraid of reaching out to others to gain insight or to simply share how your progress is going.

Body: This is still a positive card even in reverse. Being healthy and happy shouldn't deplete your bank account, so do what you can to achieve that balance in diet, exercise, and overall wellness. Take things slowly and mindfully, enjoying the journey along the way while giving yourself credit for how far you've come.

Money: Beware of comparing your financial situation or professional progress with anyone else. Think about what it's going to take to make you feel truly secure and fulfilled in the long-term, not what other people are doing or saying. If you find that a professional situation is no longer rewarding, perhaps it's time to explore other options.

Meditations: Are you exercising gratitude for all that you have right now? Are you trusting in the Universe when it comes to manifestation? Are you putting forth the right amount of effort or delegating all the work to other people?

2 Of Pentacles

Overview: Two of Pentacles indicates a balance of work and pleasure. You may have the ability to juggle more than you thought possible, but this is temporary. This is an important time to focus on maintaining a positive attitude amid any undesirable circumstances. If you persist in maintaining a positive outlook success will be yours. Two of Pentacles also indicates needing to focus on fulfilling your responsibilities to achieve long term success. This is a time to make sure that you're doing what you're supposed to and balancing your life accordingly.

Love: You may have difficulty in balancing your responsibilities and romance, leaving you feeling drained and without any extra energy for love. Your focus might also be in too many directions at once. If you're in a relationship, be sure to make quality time with your partner and vice versa. This is not time to be complacent with those you love. If you're single, you might be multitasking so much that you don't have much time at all for a partner or are experiencing difficulty in spending quality time where both of you are truly present. If you're not ready to take the romantic leap, don't push it. Allow for things to happen naturally and when you're genuinely ready, be prepared to give as much as you receive.

Mind & Spirit: Now might be an ideal time to consider how you're spending your time and how much you're devoting to your spiritual life. You might be juggling way too many things at once, leaving you with little time to nurture your own spirit. Feel free to take a step back and reconsider your priorities. If you feel like you're way too busy to take a few minutes for meditation, think about how much more overwhelmed you would be without taking that time to be mindful and centered.

Body: You might be experiencing difficulties in balancing your personal and professional life, which may be impacting your health. Be sure that you're taking enough time for self-care and taking care of your overall wellness. This card is simply a reminder to do your best to balance your overall life to ensure that you feel your best. Prioritize your health and the outcomes will be worthwhile.

Money: 30,000 is a key figure. This is a time to balance out your professional and personal life. Perhaps you've been going for some time without a vacation or tending to your personal needs. Reevaluate what it's going to take to keep you happy in the long-term, and how you will achieve that in terms of your financial goals. This is not an ideal time to get overwhelmed through persistent multitasking, but you might also find that your finances are balancing out. This is not a time to take any major risks or to scatter your energies. Seek out helpful advice if needed.

Travel: You may take a trip where you might struggle to balance both personal and professional responsibilities. If you're gonna do any juggling, be sure to juggle fun activities.

Geography: Central Africa, Polynesia

Locations: Circuses, carnivals, or arcades.

2 Of Pentacles Reversed

Overview: Two of Pentacles in reverse indicates that you may need greater organization quite soon or even more problems will manifest. Two of Pentacles in reverse also indicates losing focus as a result of financial or material loss. This is a warning to keep up on everyday responsibilities and or bills. Otherwise, problems could potentially snowball.

Love: If you're experiencing ongoing stress so much that it's impacting your interpersonal relationships, then it's time to take a break. Try to make time to do something fun to relax and unwind. This is a time to destress and to also tend to your romantic relationships if you're already committed as your energies might have become so scattered, leaving your loved one to feel neglected. If you're single, make sure that you're taking enough time to think about what it is that you really want before embarking upon a new relationship. Be realistic about your expectations and be sure about what you're looking for in terms of romance.

Mind & Spirit: As a result of multitasking, you might find yourself feeling completely overwhelmed. This is a time to reprioritize and get grounded. Your goal should be rest and rejuvenation. Any amount of effort, no matter how small, will be beneficial to you at this time.

Body: When it comes to health you might be experiencing symptoms of a head cold or flu-like symptoms. You may want to examine your vitamin and nutrition intake. Try to be careful when consuming salty foods. Monitor your salt intake as well as overall eating habits.

Money: You may find that multitasking over the long term has become too overwhelming. Before saying yes to any new project or endeavor, be sure that you've taken enough time for yourself to reflect on what it is that you need and what it's going to take for you to feel happy and secure in the long term. It's OK to say no. If you go ahead and commit to too many side projects, you'll find that you're not able to do any one of them well. When it comes to financial management, be sure that you're in control of your spending habits and not indulging in champagne taste with a beer budget.

Meditations: Are you taking time for pleasurable activities? Are you being hypersensitive to the criticism of others? Are you allowing the opinions of others make too much of an impact on you?

3 Of Pentacles

Overview: The Three of Pentacles indicates creativity and mastery. At this time, you can look forward to minimal problems from enemies. There will also be new opportunities for learning as well as enlightening experiences. This is a great time to express your creative abilities as such activities and ventures will be rewarded in the short-term. Two and four are significant numbers. Three of Pentacles indicates collaborating to achieve a common goal. This is not a time to let fear take the wheel. This might also indicate that you could benefit from seeking out a professional or mentor to achieve your goal.

Love: If you're curious as to how someone feels about you, then Three of Pentacles is an auspicious omen. If you're single and looking, then you are likely to find romance through your current profession or through some aspect of professional development events. If you're currently in a relationship, this card indicates positive feelings towards you. If you're working on communication and intimacy, just be patient with yourself and the other person involved.

Mind & Spirit: New opportunities to learn about spirituality or psychic abilities are about to manifest by examining ancient practices or rituals. You are likely to uncover new knowledge that will be beneficial to you for your spiritual journey. This will require a little investigation, but not too much effort. There is a lot of information at your disposal at this time, and no drastic measures need to be taken.

Body: You may be expecting communication or messaging regarding your health and wellness. You can anticipate good news, but this will likely come from all the effort that you put in to get healthier. Keep up the great work and maintain a positive mindset.

Money: You have the potential to make money through artisan work or other creative talents that bestow financial rewards. Have faith in your skills and talents, it will surely pay off in the long-term. This card also indicates that you're well-respected and admired within your profession. When it comes to your finances, this card indicates success after hard work and seeing a good payoff after you've put in the time to realize your goals. If you're working on a hobby or a talent, and you would like to see it bring extra income, just be patient with yourself and in time you're likely to see a positive return.

Travel: You are likely to take a trip where your skills and talents will be on display for those who appreciate your work.

Geography: Central Africa, New Caledonia

Locations: Fashion show, art exhibit, upscale shops, or museums.

3 Of Pentacles Reversed

Overview: Three of Pentacles in reverse indicates that you may need to become more responsible toward everyday tasks. Try not to start or do anything without completely understanding it or it will lead to frustration. You may have a lot of different ideas bubbling underneath the surface but it's important to take time and pace yourself. Plan ahead and think things through because if you end up acting prematurely, you're only going to wind up with more disappointment. Try not to work too hard or force anything into fruition. Enjoy the process of what you're passionate about. Three of Pentacles in reverse indicates dysfunction in partnerships or team projects where delicate egos are involved. Whether it's in the work environment or home, you might not be feeling heard or respected. If you need to change a place of residence or workplace, now is the time to weigh your options.

Love: When it comes to love, you may feel that your voice isn't being heard or that your boundaries are being tested. You may be dealing with a fragile ego and the stress of partnership is calling for a timeout to figure out both of your priorities. If you're single, you might find that professional networking is a great way to meet new people, or a colleague may try to set you up. Before starting anything new, be sure you've taken time to know and love yourself better in order to avoid repeating any unhealthy romantic patterns.

Mind & Spirit: Be careful that on the path to your spiritual development that you aren't trying to break the bank in the process. Also, be wary of any spiritual advisor who is looking for significant payment up front. Often the best advisors help us find the answers that we already hold within, and do not require that you go into debt to achieve your spiritual goals.

Body: Be careful that financial worry doesn't start to affect your health. If you're feeling burned out and overwhelmed, this is a great time to tend to self-care and do something nice for yourself.

Money: You might be feeling pessimistic lately when it comes to money. In your professional life, you might be feeling like you're overqualified for your current position. You might also have difficulty in relying on others around you in your workplace or are having difficulty and relying on anyone helping you to change your position. This is not a time to become complacent, but to do your best to ensure that you are planning your future according to your Higher Self. When it comes to other professional endeavors., be sure that you're being as diplomatic as possible in the workplace. Don't give into any workplace drama. Your finances at this time will be impacted in proportion to how much effort you put into it.

Meditations: Are you working too hard without any breaks? Are you taking the time to explore new and fun activities? Are you taking things too seriously? Are you lacking focus?

4 Of Pentacles

Overview: Four of Pentacles indicates self-reliance and practical endeavors. This is a time to rely upon yourself, trusting your own intuition, and not paying too much attention to the opinions of others. If you want your goals and dreams to manifest, do your best to keep all of it a secret until it happens. Springtime and autumn for ideal seasons but be careful not to act too aggressively with others and you will see goals come into fruition within six months' time. Four of Pentacles indicates feelings of scarcity or a mindset of lack. Despite your circumstances you might have difficulty truly experiencing joy. If you're fearing loss, this might be a time to shift your mindset or else you risk manifesting something that you don't want to happen.

Love: If you're feeling uncertain about a romantic relationship, this is a time to release any and all anxieties and allow things to flow naturally. You might have recently let go of a potential partnership or a relationship and are unsure as to whether or not you did the right thing. However, this is an indication that if something is meant to work out that it will in its own time. Be patient and trust in the Universe. If you are currently involved with someone, you might be smothering them, or they might be smothering you. Love requires trust and honoring boundaries. If you or someone else is attempting to be controlling, this is a time to be accountable to it. Genuine love does not require manipulation. If you're single, you might need to put in a bit more effort in meeting someone new. Don't expect love to appear out of thin air.

Mind & Spirit: This is a time to release all beliefs and thought patterns that no longer serve your higher purpose. Sometimes stepping away from the familiar can lead you to greater independence and self-reliance. Do not allow fear to hold you into the status quo in crippling you in the present. Understand how energy moves through you. And can get stagnant in certain areas. Seek additional guidance as needed.

Body: This is generally a good card when it comes to healing but we you must be proactive and holistically address problems in real time. Building muscle tone or working on it is ideal. Even if you look like you're carrying a few extra pounds, you're likely to be quite athletic.

Money: You might be in a situation where you are feeling like you are merely working to live and to get by. This doesn't leave much room for satisfaction. If you're looking for something that is truly fulfilling, you're going to have to put yourself out there. And take your skills to another level. Think about the ideal situation that would truly be fulfilling for you. What does that look like? When it comes to matters of finance, you might be clinging to outdated ideas or things that you've always done.

Travel: You are likely to take a trip that will force you to step outside of your comfort zone.

Geography: Central Africa, Fiji

Locations: Safes, panic rooms, or bunkers.

4 Of Pentacles Reversed

Overview: Four of Pentacles in reverse may indicate that there will be delays in plans and possible miscommunications. Pay close attention to everything and everyone around you to be sure that there are no secrets or concealing of truths. This is a time to re-evaluate things and make new plans because there may be issues when it comes to your old endeavors. This is an especially important time to build upon self-reliance and to trust your inner voice and express it accordingly. You might not be at the capacity to do everything on your own at this time and maybe you need about four to six months. If you're working on something in autumn, you're likely to see the outcome in manifestation in spring. Four Pentacles in reverse indicates a fear of material loss or having issues with relinquishing control. This might also indicate that your fears are holding you back from enjoying everything that you currently have.

Love: If you're currently in a relationship, the Four of Pentacles in reverse could be a sign of codependence. Whether you're single or attached, this is not a time to be controlling or to allow others to try to control you. You might be holding onto relationships or potential partnerships out of a sense of fear, or you may have a fear of rejection. Anyone involved in a relationship, or a potential partnership, needs to have the freedom to make their own choices. If you do follow through and allow for everybody to have a say so, then you're likely to experience greater levels of intimacy and communication.

Mind & Spirit: Don't allow fear to hold you back from making great spiritual strides. This card is not an absolute, but advice to let go of fear-based thinking. If you have the courage to do that, then wonderful things can manifest.

Body: Your health may be affected by financial difficulties. Overall, it appears that if you're experiencing health difficulties, that stress plays an important part. It might be helpful to speak with someone about all the things that are causing you additional stress. Once you do that, you might start to notice improvements.

Money: This card indicates caution regarding personal finance and investment. When Four of Pentacles is in reverse, you might have difficulty realizing the value of money. As a result of risk-taking in finances, you might experience a loss or financial set back. Be careful not to spend too much or to participate in gambling. If you're inexperienced in investing or in your current professional position, this is a time to seek out helpful guidance. This card also indicates a decrease in the value of property or real estate.

Meditations: Are you being too aggressive? Are you really seeing the truth? Are you relying on your own skill or the resources of others?

5 Of Pentacles

Overview: The Five of Pentacles indicates that it's time to examine your life lessons. Take care that all paperwork is properly addressed and scrutinized for details and catches. You will need to prepare for tougher times ahead. Three to four days, three to four months, or three to four years are time periods indicated by this card. In the meantime, it's important to plant as many seeds as you can to plan for the future. This is the time to have many options going at once. Do your best to ensure that your living environment is squared away and properly kept. This is a card that often indicates disorder and misfortune. Disorganized surroundings often equal a disorganized life. Five of Pentacles indicates a recent loss or an upcoming loss. However, this is also a card that reminds you to take your focus off the material world and go within. Take comfort in positive relationships in your life and all that you must be grateful for to help you shift your perspective from loss and lack toward gratitude in abundance. Mindset has a lot to do with this card.

Love: This card is often associated with loss and feelings of lack. Perhaps your love life is not where you'd like it to be and is causing a great deal of distress as a result. If you're single, you may feel like you're out in the cold watching others be warmed by love's glow. Know that this, too, will pass. If you're currently in a relationship, this is about reevaluating your worth and happiness if you're feeling unfulfilled. Love doesn't require a significant amount of pain, but room to grow and flourish with kindness, compassion, and mutual support. Think about all the things that you bring into a relationship and remember that you are worthy of love.

Mind & Spirit: This is not a time to rely on your intuition alone, but to be extremely organized. Your goals can be accomplished but in baby steps. Your perception and intuition might be heightened right now, but it's extremely important at this time to be organized and to plan ahead. If you're feeling alone or that luck is simply not on your side, reach out to friends and loved ones for support or even a professional to help you get back on track to a healthier, positive mindset.

Body: You may be keeping on excess weight due to stress. It's imperative to seek out stress-reducing activities to help you achieve a sense of balance, and to not give up on your health. Seek out professional guidance.

Money: Work, finances, and employment opportunities can be a significant source of stress right now. You may be feeling helpless in finances or stuck in a status quo that is now causing distress. Professional endeavors might also be delayed, and opportunities could be lost. Remember to reach out for help when you need it and don't try to go it alone. In time, things will improve.

Travel: Travel is not advised and if you proceed, be prepared for uncomfortable setbacks.

Geography: Central Africa, Vanuatu, Papua New Guinea, Solomon Islands

Locations: Streets, homeless areas, halfway houses, or shelters.

5 Of Pentacles Reversed

Overview: Five of Pentacles in reverse indicates that is time to pay attention to detail and that you might not be seeing the forest for the trees. Try not to get too nitpicky that you lose sight of the bigger picture. Remember that problems often come in the form of life lessons. They teach us to adapt and to overcome in creative new ways. If you don't take time to process and learn the lessons of the past will repeat itself. Five of Pentacles in reverse indicates a period of financial trouble is coming to an end. This is also a time to make of list of gratitude. There is much to be thankful for and know that any obstacle or trouble is temporary.

Love: Be sure that you're not neglecting someone you love or someone you plan to incorporate into your romantic life. This is a time to examine potential unhealthy romantic cycles. If you're dealing with a karmic situation, and asking yourself when the pain will stop, remember that you're the teacher and the pain will stop when you say it will. When you take the time to put yourself first and open yourself up to love, you might find that so many of your fears really stood in the way of your happiness. It's time to step out of survival mode and into thriving mode.

Mind & Spirit: You're moving from an era of survival mode into a more secure chapter where you can level-up in your spiritual life. Reaching out and connecting with others can help reduce feelings of hopelessness or isolation. You're not alone on this journey! Be grateful for those who love you and are cheering you on.

Body: You might be experiencing improvements in your health as a result of reducing stress. Be sure that you are eating right, sleeping enough, and taking care of yourself.

Money: Financial and professional opportunities start to come up and offer you a chance to improve your lot in life. An era of financial worry is coming to an end, and you might find yourself slowly moving out of the darkness and into a new chapter that offers security and stability.

Meditations: Are you neglecting everyday responsibilities? Are you not looking at the big picture? Are you getting lost in fantasies and neglecting real life? Are you failing to see what's right in front of you? Are you scattering your energies instead of harnessing your power?

6 Of Pentacles

Overview: Six of Pentacles indicates reclaiming personal power and harvesting the rewards of hard work. This is a great time to channel your own intuition via mysticism and other metaphysical means. All the patience that you've had before is about to be rewarded and you must take action when the opportunity appears. This is a time to trust in your own instincts and not to rely on people who think they know what's best for you. This is not a time to share any details about your future plans. If you do, opportunities might pass you by. You'll also find that opportunities are coming in from different directions. This is a time to reclaim your power, to rejuvenate yourself after loss, and realize that you have the ability to succeed way more than you imagined. Six of Pentacles indicates that this is a time of giving or receiving help as an investment. While there is a sense of compassion, any offers can come with strings attached. This could be you or someone who you could be dealing with, however, examine all your options and evaluate what's worth the risk.

Love: This card speaks to equality and fairness in relationships. If you're in a relationship, you might be experiencing a time of balance and calm for the time being. If you're single, you may be meeting someone through a mutual friend who strikes you as kind-hearted and giving. Generosity in a relationship can be material, spiritual, or tending to specific love language needs. Ensure that relationships are well-balanced with partners giving and taking equally. Security isn't just about money, but about providing quality time, words of affirmation, and emotional support in its various forms.

Mind & Spirit: You may feel that you're at the beginning of a hero's quest and realize that you are more powerful and capable lately. This is a time that you find you're able to tap into different dimensions. This is a great time to invest in developing your own intuitive gifts.

Body: Pay attention to issues relating to your temporal lobe. You may benefit from outdoor activities such as climbing, running, or swimming. Engaging in physical activity, especially while enjoying nature is ideal.

Money: Opportunities for financial abundance will appear very soon. If you're looking to advancing your career, this is a great time to keep an eye out for new opportunities coming your way. But you must act on it, plan for it, in seize it while it's hot. This is also a time to reciprocate generosity. If you've been fortunate, it's time to express gratitude and share your abundance with others. If you've been struggling, this is a time to step back to regain perspective.

Travel: You may be taking a trip that involves a generous gift or you may be surprising someone else with a wonderful quick getaway.

Geography: Mexico, Central America, Greater Antilles, northern Lesser Antilles, Central Africa, Australia

Locations: Cash advance sites, pawn shops, or charities.

6 Of Pentacles Reversed

Overview: The Six of Pentacles in reverse indicates that you must be cautious about others taking your power from you. You must be alert and on your guard about people intentionally putting obstacles in your way or taking opportunities away from you. Circumstances around you are not what they seem and if you ignore red flags you are bound to wind up greatly disappointed. It is likely that others around you may be jealous and consciously undermining your efforts. It also might be your own insecurity stopping you from your accomplishments. Be sure that no one including yourself is trying to sabotage your happiness. Six of Pentacles in reverse indicates an imbalance in a partnership or relationship, or that someone may be taking advantage of you. If it's been all given and no take or vice versa, it's time to step back and re-evaluate your position.

Love: You may be dealing with gaslighting in a current relationship or a potential romantic partner. Instead of second-guessing yourself, go with your intuition and trust your inner voice. Someone who may be claiming to support you and your goals maybe trying to sabotage your efforts. You or someone you care about may be stubborn about asking for or receiving help. Be willing to share your feelings and listen to others in an open and compassionate way. It's also okay to make yourself vulnerable with others, so long as you're getting the same in return.

Mind & Spirit: You may be seeking a way to balance your mind and spirit. Be careful of codependent energies or emotional vampires. Remember that the path to enlightenment is not linear.

Body: Pay attention to the signals your body is sending you. This is not a time to be passive in taking care of yourself, but to trust your senses and respond accordingly.

Money: You may feel that you're not being properly compensated for your work or talents. This is not a good time to either hoard resources or take out any loans that you cannot pay back in the short-term. Any investments or professional endeavors at this time may come with strings attached so be careful about proceeding until you've read the fine print.

Meditations: Are you trying to push too hard on your plans? Are you giving your power away? Are you allowing the past to paralyze you in the present? Are you being too impatient on the path to success? Are you overreacting instead of processing information?

7 Of Pentacles

Overview: the Seven of Pentacles is about trusting your own either into rhythms or cycles. This is also in reference to lunar cycles, in your if you're looking to manifest any goal in the short-term, it may manifest within 28 days. This card is also about the ability to adapt and overcome. If you're unsure of what to do next it's perfectly fine to stand still and not act. This is not a time to force any action, and within a month you're likely to get our answers. Once opportunities make themselves known, you can then jump on it. In the meantime, do your best to be patient. Seven of Pentacles indicates thinking about where to properly invest your time and energy. This is also an indication of focusing on long-term objectives instead of short-term wins or get-rich-quick schemes.

Love: You or someone you love may be talking about having children. This is a time of fertility so be mindful of any decisions you make. You've invested a lot in previous or current relationships and soon you're likely to receive rewards for your positive energy. If you're in a relationship right now, this is a time of good vibes and communication. If you are single and looking, consider ways to expand your horizons in order to allow for new experiences and possibilities. Be selective, but also intentional with your energies.

Mind & Spirit: If you've been working on a project pertaining to spirituality or mindfulness, this is a good time to seek out feedback. You may have recently been distracted or sidetracked in pursuit of your goals. If something isn't manifesting as you've expected, try to look at things from a different perspective. It's okay if everything isn't perfect but know that you can make adjustments along the way to perfect your goals.

Body: You may be struggling with a new wellness or fitness regimen. Perhaps your progress isn't going how you thought it would but don't lose hope. You may benefit from seeking out additional information or guidance to tweak your current routine.

Money: You might be experiencing a bit of déjà vu at this time regarding financial or professional endeavors. Are you repeating old patterns in decision-making and planning? If so, it's time to take a step back and reconsider your options and goals. This is a time of seeing returns on investments, so if you've been working hard towards a goal, you'll soon see the rewards. Congratulate yourself on your progress and connect with others who share similar goals and values.

Travel: This is an ideal time to take a short trip to re-evaluate your priorities and take a break from routine.

Geography: Central Africa, Australia

Locations: Orchards, plant nurseries, gardens, farmland, or fields.

7 Of Pentacles Reversed

Overview: Seven of Pentacles in reverse indicates that you might need to take a defensive posture. Have a plan A, B, C, D and so on. If you're in the process of putting plans into action this is a time to double-check everything. Make sure all your t's are crossed and your i's are dotted. This might be a time to pull back on current efforts to avoid potential problems. Pulling back will save you a lot of heartache. You might find that you feel out of alignment with your natural rhythm. This is a time to go within and reevaluate what it is that you want. Be specific and as detailed as possible in defining what success means to you and how to achieve a sense of fulfillment on your own terms.

Love: Seven of Pentacles in reverse indicates that you've been putting a lot of time and energy into a partnership that is not generating the rewards or outcome that you've expected. Listen to your Higher Self, and if it's time to cut your losses and walk away, it might be time to do just that. Consider the deeper meanings of fulfillment in interpersonal relationships and be realistic about your romantic relationships.

Mind & Spirit: This is a time for introspection. You may feel a bit hopeless after your efforts seem to bear few, if any, rewards. However, there's a deeper lesson to consider here. This is about reevaluating old patterns and cycles, to absorb the lessons and do away with the outdated modes of thinking and doing. It's time to truly learn from the past and be present so you don't have to fret as much about the future.

Body: You may need to reevaluate your priorities when it comes to your physical health. Examine your overall routine and think about where you can make improvements.

Money: Try not to pigeonhole yourself when it comes to your career or financial endeavors. When it comes to your professional life, you may be experiencing a lack of fulfillment or may be searching for a deeper sense of purpose. This is not a time to make rash decisions, but to sit down and truly think about what matters. When you invest this time in yourself, you're likely to see the rewards of prioritizing your needs and long-term goals. Think of your retirement goals, and not just about what you can earn in the coming year. This is a time to look at the bigger picture of stability and security.

Meditations: Are you exercising patience? Are you keeping your plans to yourself? Have you thought about alternative options?

8 Of Pentacles

Overview: Eight of Pentacles is about preparing for the future. This is a reminder that if you are doing your best to lay the foundation for the future that you're on the right track. Doing so will enable you to succeed and be comfortable in the long-term. This is all about perseverance so be alert and don't allow others to distract you from your goals. This is a time to develop effective communication skills because they will come in handy when it comes to putting your plans into action. Eight of Pentacles indicates that you might be partaking in a course or learning a new skill that will allow you to become a subject matter expert. Through a lot of hard work and dedication you will find that success is truly deserved and all the difficulties you've overcome were worthwhile.

Love: Professional responsibilities may be interfering with a current relationship or romantic pursuits. Regardless of relationship status, it will be quite important to put forth the effort and for others to do the same. Fairness and a sense of balance is required for long-term relationship success.

Mind & Spirit: It's imperative to consider if you're pursuing your life's purpose or biding your time. If you're not growing as a person, it might be time to seek alternate routes to enlightenment. Spend time making lists of short-term and long-term goals and makes plans to follow through. Be sure that what you're doing aligns with your Higher Self.

Body: It's time to be proactive with your health. This is a time of introspection and long-term planning for your wellness. Remember that you are your best advocate.

Money: This is a time of putting in labor and dedication to manifest your financial or professional goals. However, it will be important to you that the work is personally satisfying and meaningful. You're focused on a life purpose rather than just a job. You would like to be rewarded for your labor and your talents – and rightfully so! Persevere and continue your labors of love and in the end, you shall find both the process and the outcome quite rewarding.

Travel: You may be taking a trip to acquire a new skill or experience that will play into your long-term goals.

Geography: Central Africa, Australia

Locations: Wood workshops or artisan shops.

8 Of Pentacles Reversed

Overview: Eight of Pentacles in reverse indicates that you might be taking on too much at one time. Make sure that you're balancing work and play. You also might be going about your plans the wrong way and require guidance from an expert in that field. This is a time for work not for quick and easy shortcuts. Re-evaluate your long-term plans and decide what it's going to take for you to be happy. Eight of Pentacles in reverse indicates that perfectionism might be hindering your progress. You might be like laser-focused on tiny details instead of looking at the whole picture. Take a step back to see the forest for the trees.

Love: Body language and nonverbal communication are things you should pay attention to when it comes to matters of the heart. Are messages and conversations corresponding with actions? There may also be too much noise in the home or chaos which could be impacting your love life. If you're in a relationship, you may find that someone isn't exactly pulling their weight and it must be addressed. If not, resentment will cause problems. Whether attached or single, beware of freeloaders looking to take advantage of your hard work and generosity. If you persevere in solving problems in your romantic life you will succeed. Remember that your success doesn't have to look like anyone else's though.

Mind & Spirit: A person, resource, or opportunity you were counting on to improve your life might've fallen through. Do not despair as the setback is only a temporary one. You have more power to change your circumstances than you realize.

Body: This is an important time to take a breather and engage in much needed self-care. You might find that a brief break from routine could be energizing to your health and wellbeing.

Money: It is possible that you are putting too much emphasis on work and neglecting your personal life. If you're looking to make any investments, be sure to think about long-term consequences and repercussions before deciding. Avoid any money-making opportunities that seem way too good to be true – because they probably are. If you're looking for a new career or position, this is an auspicious time to make a wonderful impression. If you're happy with what you're currently doing, keep going. Complacency and delusions are your enemies right now, so be vigilant and mindful in all matters of professional opportunities and finance.

Meditations: Are you looking for quick fixes instead of long-term solutions? Are you making enough time for everyday pleasures? Are you running yourself into the ground?

9 Of Pentacles

Overview: Nine of Pentacles is about working for your dreams. However, hopes, dreams, and plans take hard work. There is a strong sense of security in what you're doing, and you might find yourself in a position where you are more knowledgeable than others. This is a time to manifest dreams as it pertains to home life and family. Do what you can to act upon your goals right now and you will see that within a year's time many of your efforts manifest. For the next year, get to work on making those dreams come true. Nine of Pentacles indicates the need to control one's emotions. It also represents being very close to completing a goal or project that will turn out wonderful once it's done. This is a card the indicates wealth and a luxurious lifestyle that is also emotionally fulfilling.

Love: A secure home life is indicated with the Nine of Pentacles and for good reason. This card is about bestowing love, comfortable surroundings, and providing long-term security. If you're currently in a relationship, this bodes well for a calm and cozy home life that entertains your love languages. If you're single, a new love interest will emerge and may present all that you've been looking for in love and intimacy. Enjoy this time and notice the beauty around you.

Mind & Spirit: You're in an ideal position to achieve your spiritual goals. This is a time to take control of your destiny by mapping your future as you have the power of manifestation in your hands. You deserve a wonderful day so treat yourself to a massage or anything that relaxes you.

Body: This is a positive sign for overall health and wellness. If you have any concerns, you're likely to find the right information and answers to your questions. Maintain a positive mindset and continue doing your very best.

Money: If you've been concerned about money, this card indicates that financial or professional stressors are coming to an end, allowing an era of fulfillment and joy to take place. Be sure to express gratitude for all blessings bestowed upon you and share your positive energy with others as they develop their talents and manifest their dreams.

Travel: You are likely to take a luxurious vacation after a period of hard work and putting your talents to good use. You may bring friends, loved ones, or family members to enjoy the fruits of your labor.

Geography: Central Africa, Australia

Locations: A well-kept garden and topiary mazes.

9 Of Pentacles Reversed

Overview: When Nine of Pentacles is in reverse it indicates that there might not be enough action corresponding with our aspirations. It's time to get your head out of the clouds and do the needed work. There could also be issues with unnecessary arguments or interpersonal drama. Nine of Pentacles in reverse indicates a potential loss due to bad decision making. You might be encountering an obstacle or expect to live a life of luxury without having put the work into it. This is a time to check your ego and ask yourself if your goals truly align with your Higher Self.

Love: You may feel as though you're not getting the love and reciprocation you deserve in your romantic life. If you want to deepen intimacy in a current relationship or engage in a new romance, you have to put in the work to make it happen. Fall in love with yourself first, and then fall in love with whoever you want.

Mind & Spirit: You could be experiencing issues with your self-worth and feeling grounded in the present. While this is still a positive card, you might not notice the opportunities for growth around you. Take some time to meditate to bring yourself back into the present. This is also a sign not to overindulge in sensual pleasures.

Body: Be on the lookout for dental issues. You may need to focus on dental hygiene and care at this time.

Money: You may be spending money soon on home repair. Check around to see if anything needs mending or if a professional needs to be called. If you're looking for a new opportunity, be sure to invest the time and effort to see any payoff. This is a time to be assertive and not simply expect opportunities to appear out of thin air.

Meditations: Are you neglecting your dreams? Are you paying enough attention to your home? Are you doing the required work to achieve your goal? Is anything in your home in need of repair?

10 Of Pentacles

Overview: Ten of Pentacles is an auspicious card which also pertains to home, fertility, and generosity. This is a time of a renewed sense of security and prosperity. Energies at home are likely to be powerful. This is a card of creativity, intuition, and manifestation. This is also a card indicating providing for younger people in your life. You might have felt alone on the road to success or manifesting a dream. However, even more new accomplishments are on the horizon. Expect new opportunities to manifest in autumn. Ten of Pentacles indicates an increase in financial security an abundance. This is an indication of being rewarded for a long period of hard work that results in a much more stable future.

Love: This card is an auspicious omen for love. If you're currently in a relationship, this is a positive sign for relationship progress. It is possible to enter a relationship or a marriage for financial security. This is a time where relationships are taken to the next level whether it is cohabitating, marriage, having children, or any significant life event that will transform a relationship. If you're single, this could indicate that a new love is coming into your life that is transformative and positive. This is a grounding energy that promotes a healthy home life and financial security. This may be a bit unexpected for you, and this person may not be the type that you would typically pursue. However, keep an open mind.

Mind & Spirit: This card regarding wellbeing in spiritual life is generally quite positive. This is a great time to find your center, and a sense of grounding. This might be an optimal time to take a trip where you can expand your mind and your third eye.

Body: Your health is forecasted to go quite well when this card appears concerning physical wellbeing. You are also in a better state of mind or within reach of multiple opportunities to improve your overall health.

Money: This card indicates significant, positive changes in your financial status. This could have to do with the purchase of a new home or starting a new business. There may be an unexpected windfall which will aid you in financial security and success in financial matters altogether. Regarding professional endeavors, this card indicates a potential promotion or the opening of a new opportunity that will likely improve your financial status. This will be an enjoyable time for you personally and professionally. You may start to feel that your talents and hard work are finally being appreciated and noticed by others.

Travel: You could take a trip where an inheritance may be discussed, or the trip might be unexpected altogether.

Geography: Canada, Central Africa, Australia

Locations: Bazaars, one's own home, or outdoor parties.

10 Of Pentacles Reversed

Overview: You might be failing to see the forest for the trees. It's important to trust your inner voice and intuition. If you ignore your inner voice, you're likely to encounter more problems within a month. Beware of anything clouding your judgment. Ten of Pentacles in reverse indicates that you might experience financial loss or that a relationship may not have the long-term potential that you might have thought.

Love: Ten of Pentacles in reverse is still quite a fortuitous omen when it comes to your love life. However, it's important not to make any significant risks when it comes to your long-term financial security as it could have an impact on current or potential relationships. This could also indicate a sense of complacency in your relationship or in your love life in general. If you're feeling a bit bored, talk with your partner or a potential partner about things that you can do to awaken or reawaken romance. If you're single, this is still quite a good card, and indicates that you might need to think more realistically in terms of long-term success, long-term security, and how that relates to your romantic relationships. Remember, relationships are also an investment of time, money, and hard work. Try to see if you need to do any inner work before starting a new relationship.

Mind & Spirit: Your spiritual life should still be quite good, but you might be experiencing a sense of boredom when it comes to your ongoing spiritual routine. Be open to new opportunities having to deal with improving your spiritual life and mental wellness.

Body: Diet and nutrition is likely affecting physical and mental energy levels. Be sure that you are taking care of yourself well enough and seek out professional care.

Money: Ten of Pentacles in reverse indicates that there will be no significant changes when it comes to your financial status or your professional life. However, be on the lookout to possibly start supporting elder relatives or those needing significant help in daily living. You might also experience financial loss of an inheritance or through risky spending. If you have any current doubts about your financial situation or your professional opportunities, think logically and rationally before making any major changes. When it comes to your financial security, be especially thoughtful about who you trust when making investment decisions.

Meditations: Are you distracted? Are you ignoring your inner voice? Are you accepting a variety of red flags? Are you letting other people know your plans before they happen?

Page Of Pentacles

Overview: Page of Pentacles indicates new educational opportunities and pursuits. This is a card that indicates transformative adventures, opening eyes to new horizons, and inspiration. This indicates new opportunities for learning new skills, new educational pursuits, and invitations to take on new projects. The next five years is of upmost importance. A new awakening is coming. Page of Pentacles indicates potential upcoming travel and spending time gathering resources and knowledge to prepare for the road ahead. This energy results in manifesting dreams that previously seemed impossible.

Love: You may be feeling impulsive when it comes to love. Whether you're committed or single, you might be encountering someone who can potentially present a new love affair. Beware of succumbing to impulsive behavior, but also be open to shaking things up and having a bit of fun. Just make sure that you're being honest to anyone that you've promised your loyalty. If you're currently in a relationship, this may mean that you need to do something exciting to reinvigorate your romantic life. This is not necessarily a warning but a reminder to not become complacent in matters of the heart. If you're single and are having difficulties meeting the right people, take a step back and look at the bigger picture. If you're holding on to an old love in your heart, it may be time to let them go if you want to make room for someone new.

Mind & Spirit: If you're thinking about new and exciting ways to enrich your spiritual life, this is a great time to be open to new opportunities to make things exciting. Perhaps you've become a bit bored in your current routine. Be open to exploring new ideas, rituals, and information pertaining to improving your overall spiritual wellness.

Body: This is not a time to become complacent with your physical health. Take a look at your overall wellness from a macro perspective. If you're neglecting your physical or mental health in any way, this might be the best time to seek out professional guidance.

Money: Page of Pentacles indicates that you might be acquiring new skills that have to do with increasing your financial status or opening you up to new opportunities for work. You may be invited to summits or conferences focusing on professional development or increasing your financial status. This is the time to channel your energies into hard work to realize your financial and professional goals. This is also a time to save money rather than spend. If you're considering all your skills and talents, think about what it would take to make you feel fulfilled professionally and financially.

Travel: You may be traveling long-distance to a conference or summit where you will partner with other people to improve your life professionally or personally.

Geography: Central Africa, Australia

Locations: Conferences, summit venues, or classrooms.

Page Of Pentacles Reversed

Overview: Page of Pentacles in reverse indicates that you might have wandered off your path. Plans may experience delays or may not come to fruition at this time. Try not to push too hard for anything to manifest. For the next few days pay close attention to your inner voice and try not to expose yourself or personal information to other people. For the next year it would be advisable to work on developing your intuition. Page of Pentacles in reverse indicates that you should be careful of losing motivation and standing in your own way. This might also indicate that you might not have been as excited as you thought about a new endeavor or relationship and find yourself lacking enthusiasm.

Love: When Page of Pentacles is in reverse, you might be a bit too distracted to focus on just one person. If you're in a relationship, be careful of straying from your path of loyalty if that's what you've promised. This card indicates that love affairs are quite possible. If you're bored with your current relationship, there are many ways to reignite the flame. If you're single, you might find that you have quite a few options and are not necessarily ready for a commitment. Go with the flow for now and enjoy the ride.

Mind & Spirit: You may feel as though you're straying from your spiritual path. If you're feeling that you're stuck in somewhat of a rut, do not despair. It might be time to take a short trip out of town to recharge your spiritual batteries. Remember, that no one is perfect, and a little change now and then is quite healthy. Be open to shaking up your routine.

Body: Be careful of minor injuries or accidents while out and about and having fun. This is a time where you might get a bit too carried away, which can result in getting yourself hurt especially when substances are involved.

Money: You may be feeling overwhelmed in your professional life, and it might be time to ask others for help or to delegate certain tasks to others. Remember that you have people around you who could definitely help. When it comes to financial matters this is not a time to make any risky investments or to engage in frivolous spending or gambling. If needed contact a financial consultant to help you sort out your finances if you have a hard time setting limitations on what you do with your money.

Meditations: Are you allowing others to violate your boundaries? Are you being hypercritical of yourself? Have you wandered off your path?

Knight Of Pentacles

Overview: Knight of Pentacles indicates coming into your power with elevated self-motivation that can lead to success and genuine leadership skills. This is a card of a quick learner, to acknowledge one's own abilities and trust in them. In order to understand power, you must understand what it requires. Through trial and error, you can become knowledgeable and an expert in your field. This is a time to act quickly and strongly when opportunities arise. This is a time to be strategic and to respond immediately when threatened. Be mindful of other people's weaknesses and vulnerabilities. This is a time to express power creatively in dynamically. Knight of Pentacles indicates someone who is focused and hardworking. While this is not the fastest moving knight, this indicates someone who is logical and methodical in everything that they do and has the power to manifest real results. This could potentially be someone you work with or someone you will partner with for a successful project.

Love: Knight of Pentacles indicates that you may have a lot of energy lately that is related to sensual or sexual desires, and how it plays into your desire for financial security. You may be trying to balance romance and long-term stability, which is not a bad thing. Whether you're in a relationship or single, just remember that love and relationships take hard work. Every day will not be like a romantic comedy. There will be days of picking up dirty socks and figuring out how to pay bills together. If you're single, you might need to shake up your routine in order to make room for someone new to enter your life. Perhaps you've been sticking to the same methods of meeting someone new. This is a time to be adventurous and to be open to new possibilities.

Mind & Spirit: Something seems to be causing you anxiety lately and you might not be sure of the cause. It is likely that you're experiencing a spiritual transformation, which is not always easy to process but will open you up to a greater understanding of the Universe. If you've been searching for answers as of late, remember that you often hold those answers within already. Sometimes you need to change things up to gain a bit of perspective and look at situations from a completely different angle in order to understand your role and purpose.

Body: An abundance of energy and good health. If you're waiting for news pertaining to your physical wellness, you're likely to receive a notification of good results.

190

Money: You can anticipate good news through a variety of communication methods having to do with money. You might also hear about receiving an inheritance particularly having to do with inheriting real estate or luxury items. You may hear from a friend who is looking to repay you for money that they've borrowed from you a while ago. If you're looking for a promotion or a salary increase, this is likely in the near future. Be sure that you are projecting reliability.

Travel: You may be taking a trip where you can expand your current set of skills, or you might be attending a seminar having to do with improving motivation and focus.

Geography: Central Africa, New Zealand

Locations: Professional seminars or stables.

Knight Of Pentacles Reversed

Overview: When the Knight of Pentacles in reverse you may be acting too aggressively. It's important to know when to be assertive, when to be aggressive, and when to be balanced in your response. This is a time for diplomacy and soft power. Be careful of not abusing any power or being too impatient on the path to success or opportunities will pass by. Other people around you maybe stifling your growth, holding you back, and trying to make you comfortable with the status quo. It's important not to accept that and know that you're capable of so much more. Knight of Pentacles in reverse indicates feeling stuck in a rut, whether it's a relationship or a work environment.

Love: if you're currently in a relationship you or your partner maybe a bit too aggressive as of late. Some of the anxieties you might be feeling might have a lot to do with being stuck in a relationship rut. This is a time to shake up your routine and work on effective communication. Don't assume that people know that you love them. Be sure that's communicated on all sides. If you're single, this is a great time to have a bit of fun and to get to know people but not to get too serious. If you feel that someone is being a bit too pushy about getting serious with you, take a step back and revaluate what's happening. This could very well be a red flag.

Mind & Spirit: You might be experiencing a bit of difficulty in balancing your personal and professional life, which is, in turn, affecting your spiritual life. You may need to take a bit more time for self-care and meditation. If you're feeling uncertain about which path to take, this is a great time to reach out to someone who has been on a similar spiritual path who could provide further insight on how to get out of this current rut.

Body: Personal responsibility is key when it comes to the Knight of Pentacles in reverse regarding health. Be sure that you're taking nutrition, diet, and exercise seriously while taking enough time for self-care. Be careful of engaging in risky activity that could result in physical injuries.

Money: This is a period of hard work when it comes to your professional and financial status. This is not a time to get caught not being mindful of your work. While you may feel a bit bored or underwhelmed with your current routine, be open to exploring other options but don't make any rash decisions. You have time to process any new information before making any major life decisions.

Meditations: Are you ignoring opportunities out of fear or complacency? Are you unhappy with the status quo? Are you giving your power away to others? Are you trying to force anything to happen?

Queen Of Pentacles

Overview: The Queen of Pentacles is a card of creativity and knowledge. This is a mature energy of wonderful creative talent and self-reliance that is awakened to the hidden knowledge and mysteries of life. This is a great time to develop creative skills and to act upon opportunities accordingly. This is also an important time to be compassionate and assist others in need. Trust your inner voice and intuition because you're likely to be correct. Look for opportunities to manifest within two months. If you're looking to be self-sufficient or for opportunities where you will be working alone, you are likely to see opportunities manifest in late winter. Queen of Pentacles indicates someone with a powerful energy to comfort others around them, who is more than capable of providing, and has an abundance of compassion. This is someone who has leadership skills and the ability to make things happen. If you're looking to manifest a goal and need assistance, this is the person for you.

Love: This is about making love happen naturally. Whether you're single or in a relationship, this is a sign to take your home life seriously but also make it an oasis for peace and tranquility. If you're currently in a relationship think about all the ways that you can improve your comfort and long-term success. Your home life needs to be welcoming and free of unnecessary stressors because you deserve it. If someone is taking away from your peace, it's time to have a serious conversation about making radical changes for the better. You'll get your answer soon. However, if you're single, you need to think with your heart and your mind. It's important to partner with someone, if that's your goal, who has the same or a similar vision of the future. Remember that love is not just looking into one another's eyes, it's looking in the same direction.

Mind & Spirit: Your intuition and perceptions are much stronger at this time and it's important to focus on this especially in the winter. The mysteries and secrets that you uncover about yourself will make you more perceptive and helpful to others around you.

Body: You may be making an appointment to get an X-ray done, or you may be waiting on results pertaining to a previous radiology appointment. This is a time to prioritize your health, and not get sidetracked by too many requests for your assistance.

Money: Be on the lookout for professional opportunities or financial decisions involving blue and/or yellow logos. if you're waiting on answers pertaining to money or job opportunities, you can expect to manifest those goals within two months. You might also be looking into starting or expanding upon a home-based business that could prove lucrative in the long-term. Queen of Pentacles in this position pertains to home life, family, and long-term comfort that is achieved through smart decision-making. Remember you can achieve your goals without going into debt.

Travel: You will be taking a trip where people will be seeking out your expertise and advice on how to improve their home life or business.

Geography: Greece, Central Africa, New Zealand

Locations: Home offices, luxury furniture stores, or dental offices.

Queen Of Pentacles Reversed

Overview: The Queen of Pentacles in reverse indicates that you must be careful when it comes to trust and keeping secrets. This card indicates that information has the potential to be publicized and distorted. There might be a fear of failing because we're not seeing things clearly. The theme of this card is essentially being responsible with secrets and also uncovering the truth. It's important to be discreet especially with information that could be damaging if made public. Others around might be uncomfortable with you because they see that you could see right through them. Be careful of people who are overeager to share secrets and remember that if they're willing to tell other people's secrets they're willing to tell yours.

Love: Queen of Pentacles in reverse indicates someone who might be nitpicky or overbearing in your romantic life. This could also indicate someone who is manipulative and using fear-based tactics to get what they want which should be viewed as blaring red flags. This card encourages you to take a realistic look and be objective about your home life situation. You deserve peace and not to come home to discord. If you're single and looking, it's important that you establish a comfortable and secure home base before starting a new relationship. Make sure that you feel like your best self before opening yourself up to someone new.

Mind & Spirit: This is a time to gather your energies and focus on building a comfortable and peaceful home life to nurture your mind and spirit. This might involve renewing or creating new routines or rituals. This might also be a great time to start an affirmations list as well as one focusing on gratitude. The key right now is to invest in yourself.

Body: You may have been neglecting your physical health and wellness needs while taking care of others. It's important to take a step back and reevaluate what it is that you need to be your best self.

Money: This is a time to evaluate what happiness and fulfillment means for you both personally and professionally. If you find yourself stuck in a rut professionally, or financially, this may be a time to revisit your long-term plans and goals. Keep in mind this is not a wise time to frivolously spend or gamble. This is a time to invest in building a quality home life that is secure and stable. Remember that your path doesn't need to look like everyone else's, and the same goes for happiness.

Meditations: Are you being discreet? Are you ignoring your intuition? Are you telling secrets when you should be keeping them?

King Of Pentacles

Overview: The King of Pentacles is a card of strength, authority, and generosity. This is a card that's about giving to the community or a person who is quite intelligent. This is about being able to regulate emotions but also knowing how to demonstrate affection. It is also a confirmation that your plans, goals, and endeavors are likely to succeed. Four is a significant number. This is a time to remain grounded and to maintain responsibility. This is a card of higher status imposition that is acquired after years of hard work. You are about to be recognized for all your hard work. King of Pentacles indicates you or someone you know is experienced and lives a luxurious lifestyle. This is someone of material wealth as well as being rich with knowledge. This is someone who is very grounded with a good heart and is focused on taking care of the people around them.

Love: The King of Pentacles signifies someone who is very trustworthy, financially responsible, and serious about building a quality home life. Whether you're in a relationship or single, this is an excellent sign of someone who is grounded and capable of delivering your romantic expectations. It is of the utmost importance to be grounded at this time and transparent in all your intentions. If you're currently in a relationship, you might find an increase in comfort. This may mean moving in together or building a wonderful home life. If you have any concerns, it's important to be honest and open with the other person. If you're single, it might be in your best interest to look for someone who is quite stable and serious but also willing to love you for who you really are on the inside. Remember, that real love will never make you feel like your basic needs are too much. The right person will be happy to be there for you and support you all the way.

Mind & Spirit: This is a great time to seek out guidance in improving your overall spiritual knowledge.

Body: This is a good card that indicates the need to focus on mind and body wellness.

Money: You or someone you know might be an excellent financial advisor. This represents someone who is very practical but also very caring about others in their lives. This is a great time to seek guidance in starting a new business or building a stronger foundation for your loved ones and yourself. You might also be dealing with someone who may be older and with a bit more experience that could be of assistance to you in achieving your long-term and short-term goals. Seek out their advice when it comes to business decisions, finance, and anything having to do with sales. This is not a time to deviate from a traditional path of getting things done but seeking out the guidance of experienced people in your field.

Travel: You may be taking a trip to meet in mentor or someone who will have a lasting impact on your long-term success

Geography: Central Africa, UK, Ireland, Central Asia, US West, Belize, French Guiana, Haiti, Guyana, Suriname, Aruba, Dutch Antilles, New Zealand

Locations: Corporate offices, business consulting firms, ballrooms, or safe houses.

King Of Pentacles Reversed

Overview: King of Pentacles in reverse indicates that you might be careless in your everyday activities, and you might have become complacent with others around you. You or someone else you might know may be acting too materialistic or may view you as a threat. Look out for complications or drama resulting from envious eyes and materialistic people. This may also indicate issues with authority or that someone is trying to take charge when they are unqualified to do so. King of Pentacles in reverse indicates someone who is overly concerned with wealth and status rather than content of character.

Love: This is a strong indication not to become complacent in your romantic life. If you're currently in a relationship you might find that you or your partner might have become complacent over time. This might be due to external factors, or issues outside of the home. Be patient and compassionate with yourself and/or the other person. Think about new ways to show that you appreciate one another. If you're single, you might be meeting someone new who is successful and stable but might present a significant income gap. Remember, your identity is way more than professional titles or degrees.

Mind & Spirit: You might have been sidetracked in the recent past when it comes to feeling stable and secure. Perhaps you have overemphasized the material in your life, even on the path to spiritual enlightenment. Be open minded about learning new things and new ways to tap into your intuition and connect to your Higher Self.

Body: It's important to take time off to get a break from everyday stressors and to focus on self-care at this time. You can make significant changes to your health by simply being mindful of how you can eat, sleep, and take care of yourself in general.

Money: This is a big reminder to diversify your income streams or financial portfolio. The key to long-term financial success as well as professional success relies on a variety of factors. You might also be dealing with an older person who might be stubborn, overbearing, or stuck in their ways which may be a point of frustration when making financial decisions or embarking on new professional opportunities. If you're experiencing financial difficulties, know that this too will pass.

Meditations: Are you trying to act with authority without merit? Are you fulfilling your responsibilities to those you love and your community? Are you being too materialistic?

SWORDS

Ace Of Swords

Overview: The Ace of Swords indicates a time of new information and success. This is a time to focus on new plans as new dimensions and opportunities are opening up. Look to March as being a time for new information, messages, and prospects. This indicates that a foundation has been laid for building up on the future and new opportunities are about to manifest in ways that are unique to you. Outdated ways of doing things or thinking are over. This is a time of new innovation, abilities, and opportunities for tremendous growth. Ace of Swords indicates problem-solving, quick wit, and rapid messages. Anything having to do with public communication could be done quite well with passionate and articulate speech. This is a card of increased mental and physical strength, and the ability to overcome obstacles.

Love: This card speaks to new beginnings and new messages pertaining to your romantic life. Outdated issues in romances that have run past their expiration date are making their way out the door to make way for new beginnings. This is a time to release negative thought patterns when it comes to love. If you're currently in a relationship, you might have a few concerns about where you're headed with this person and communication is key. If you're noticing any red flags, now is the time to speak up. If you're single, you can look forward to receiving new messages regarding various romantic opportunities.

Mind & Spirit: As of late, there definitely seems to be a drum beating. This might be the optimal time to seek out a spiritual advisor who is an expert in their field. This is a great time to get more information and new insights regarding your spiritual path. You might also be feeling overwhelmed with an abundance of information at your disposal, so see what's worked for others in the past.

Body: This is an excellent time to overcome any vice that might be affecting your health in negative ways. You might also be experiencing a bit of anxiety which can be alleviated through quality self-care time. This is also an optimal time to take action regarding a fitness routine.

Money: You might be feeling a little restless in terms of your professional life and are on the fence about whether to take advantage of a new opportunity or to stay put. If you feel like your voice is not being heard, this is an excellent time to speak out and to provide your own constructive criticism in a diplomatic way. In terms of finances, this is a time to figure out your limitations. This is not a wise period to take any major risks or to gamble with your money.

Travel: You may be taking a trip where you will be featured as a public speaker, or you will be attending a seminar or workshop to listen to a public speaking engagement.

Geography: North Africa, Hawaii, Jamaica, Scandinavia, North Asia, Micronesia

Locations: Editorial offices, a writer's room, or a publishing house.

Ace Of Swords Reversed

Overview: When Ace of Swords is in reverse you might be experiencing a lack of discrimination in your everyday life. This is a warning to be both cautious and diplomatic. Try not to force or pressure anyone to do anything. When it comes to your own paperwork be sure to double and triple check for any errors or vital information that might have been missed. Be sure to do your best to plan to avoid unnecessary obstacles or further delays. Ace of Swords in reverse indicates that you might have been having trouble in completing a task due to a lack of focus.

Love: When it comes to love, the Ace of Swords in reverse indicates no new beginnings or possible issues with current romantic ties. This is a time to resolve outstanding issues or grudges you might have. You might also be feeling a bit of anxiety or fear regarding your love life. This is a great time to work on your self-esteem in to address any fears that might be standing in the way of a healthy love life. This might also indicate feeling bored or complacent in your love life and that you might be feeling stuck in deciding what to do next. If you're single, you might find yourself growing attached to someone who is covered in red flags. If someone is emotionally unavailable and tells you so, believe them.

Mind & Spirit: This is a time to be exceptionally careful in your thought processes. This might be a great time to reassess what's important for you on your path to spiritual enlightenment. You might also want to exercise caution in anyone trying to coerce you into a new belief system or organization. Beware of any spiritual guide or self-proclaimed expert who wants you to pay to play on your path to your Higher Self.

Body: Ace of Swords in reverse indicates that you might need to get a second opinion regarding your physical health. Be sure that the person that you are consulting with is qualified to speak on any issues that you're concerned about. It's in your best interest to research any new treatments or medications that may be offered to you.

Money: This is not a great time for your work environment or professional development. Sudden changes or difficulties in communication can arise when it comes to your professional endeavors or financial goals. This is a time to put yourself in other people's shoes and try to see things from different perspectives before making a decision. When it comes to making any new investments, be careful about people making mistakes intentionally or unintentionally. Double and triple check everything.

Meditations: Are you being objective about how you're feeling? Are you seeing things rationally? Is over-analysis preventing you from acting? Are you trying to do things the way they've always been done?

2 Of Swords

Overview: Two of Swords is a card about choices and exercising your own power. There will be opportunities to develop your own innate abilities. When you tap into your intuition it opens you up to a higher level of consciousness. New doors will open so long as you act appropriately. If you do make a wrong decision, it will likely lead to more complications. To avoid any potential consequences be sure that you're acting with integrity. It's important to dig deep into your own personal power and awaken latent talent. It's crucial for you to develop skills and abilities to manifest your goals. There are no shortcuts on this path to success and you must commit physically and spiritually in order to achieve. Two of Swords indicates that you are someone you know might be afraid of acting out of fear of making a mistake. You also might not be seeing the forest for the trees or the bigger picture. If you feel that a situation has not fully been explained or that someone is withholding information, be assertive and ask. Fear has a lot to do with not knowing, and much can be resolved with investigating and asking questions.

Love: This card indicates a needed adjustment in your perspective. If you're currently in a relationship, you might be looking forward to ensuring that this is an equal partnership. It's important to take everyone's wants and needs seriously at this time within reason. This is a period of achieving balance but keep in mind that no one is perfect. However, it's important to establish and enforce boundaries when needed. If you're single, this is a great time for introspection. If you're dealing with a lot of unresolved trauma, understand that this can attract the wrong person who is looking to manipulate someone who is wounded. Keep in mind that regardless of your relationship status that it is important to be whole before you meet a partner. The best person to show up in your life and change your perspective is you. Have a wonderful relationship with yourself first and then open yourself up to opportunities.

Mind & Spirit: This is a great time to carve out your own path when it comes to your own spiritual enlightenment. Keep in mind that not everybody's path is the same, and part of the fun is figuring out what works best for you.

Body: It's important to keep in mind how stress and anxiety can impact your mental health. In turn, and over the long-term, stress can impact your physical health. This might be an ideal time to start a bullet journal and figure out patterns in your life that are connected to your overall wellness.

Money: You might be standing at a crossroads regarding your financial decisions and professional life. Do your best to be accountable, and make sure everyone else around you is doing the same.

Travel: You may take a trip or you're going to have to make a long-term life decision that will be directly tied to your long-term happiness.

Geography: Polynesia

Locations: Oceanfront locations, basements, or abandoned houses.

2 Of Swords Reversed

Overview: When Two of Swords is in reverse it's a reminder to follow through on any plans or projects. Leaving any loose ends behind are likely to come back and haunt you. You must make decisions and act assertively. This is a time to master your energies and skills instead of dabbling in a variety of fields. You or someone around you might be getting involved in things that they shouldn't, and you must be careful. Two of Swords in reverse indicates and increase in indecision. Perhaps there are way too many options or too much information leaving you feeling more confused than ever. Take a moment to sit down and think about which option or outcome would be best for you for anyone involved.

Love: Two of Swords reverse indicates a lack of self-awareness or refusal to see the truth in your romantic life. Maybe there are some issues that you are refusing to face and are resorting to fantasy-based thinking. This is not a time to fall in love with potential. However, not all hope is lost. In order to resolve any romantic issues whether you're in a relationship or single, this is a time to go within and trust your intuition rather than fear-based thinking.

Mind & Spirit: This is a time to focus on your own spiritual path instead of getting distracted by what everybody else is doing. It's important to use logic and try to understand your path from a macro perspective. This is not a time to lose yourself in someone else's identity.

Body: This is the time to take it easy regarding your physical health. This is not a time to take any drastic measures when it comes to your overall wellness.

Money: This is a time to be open and receptive to the insights and opinions of others regarding your finances in professional life. Instead of trying to go it alone, this is a time to partner up with others on the path to success. Exercise caution when placing your trust in anyone handling your finances.

Meditations: Are you or other people around you abusing your abilities? Are you trying to be a Jack-of-all-trades? Are you acting impulsively without thinking?

3 Of Swords

Overview: Three of Swords appears to be about heartbreak but it's also about the healing of the heart. This is a time to take off rose-colored lenses and to stop avoiding processing painful memories. This is a time to heal heartaches whether it's from loved ones or family and to resolve old issues, settle disputes, and start the healing process. This is a time to end karmic cycles willfully and to begin the healing process so that you may have a heart that is prepared to love. Remember that sorrow is a temporary emotion, and the pain won't last forever. Three of Swords also indicates that there's no running away from this unhappiness. However, many of these difficult life lessons provide invaluable insight an incredible growth. This is a time to sit with the grief and ask yourself what it would take for you to be happy and to heal.

Love: The Three of Swords often refers to betrayal, loss, and heartache. While this is an ominous card to get regarding romantic relationships, it indicates that you may be at a breaking point in a current relationship or in your romantic life in general. You might be in a situation where someone you trusted turns out to be a completely different person. This is an indication to prepare to move forward in a direction of self-love, with or without this person. In any case, there seems to be a significant loss of trust with a loved one and while it might be difficult to see a positive way forward, just remember that the pain that you may be experiencing now may be a catalyst for a bright new chapter ahead. What's important is to keep moving forward and to love yourself. If you've had issues with putting yourself first before, now is the time to address any codependent behaviors or if you're dealing with abuse.

Mind & Spirit: You may benefit from sound therapy or alternative approaches to processing painful or traumatic memories. This is not a time to keep dwelling on your pain and staring in the rearview mirror. It's okay to look back at the past, just don't unpack and live there. This is a time to consider what might be holding you back, and what it's going to take to release your grip on the past.

Body: Wallowing in sadness or untreated mental health conditions may be impacting your physiological health. This is not a time to ignore your inner voice but to pay attention to what your body is saying with love and compassion.

Money: Exercise caution with professional endeavors and personal finances. This might be an era of disappointment but do not fret. Avoid workplace drama, and if you're dealing with a recent major disappointment, take a step back and reevaluate your goals. Figure out what your next steps are going to be to push you in the most positive direction possible. Things might be a bit overwhelming at this time, so it may be advisable to seek out professional assistance.

Travel: You may be taking a trip where your priority is to end a relationship, a partnership, or to deal with the loss.

Geography: Central America, South America, New Caledonia

Locations: Psychotherapy offices, recovery centers, or rainforests.

3 Of Swords Reversed

Overview: Three of Swords in reverse indicates that past wounds have become a pattern in your life. You might also be considering karma carried over from past lives and how to resolve it. Remember that healing and forgiveness starts with you and that if you attempt to foster peace it may provide a solid foundation to breaking old patterns that are no longer beneficial to you. Sometimes it's helpful to look at the past to understand the present. However, you must be careful to not stare into the past so long that you unpack and live there. Three of Swords in reverse indicates that you or someone you might know is having a difficult time letting go of the past. If you're currently dealing with holding a grudge this is a time to let it go. Ask yourself if anything is holding you back from living the life that you truly want. Find a way to express this grief or loss or talk to someone you trust. You can't see the road ahead of you if you're constantly staring in the rearview mirror.

Love: You might have given up on a recent relationship or potential romantic partnership. You might also be seeing the light of the end of the tunnel after a significant loss or after experiencing betrayal. You might not be seeing all the benefits at this time but part of you knows that the only way is up from here. You may be stuck in a mode where you feel like nothing ever really works out for you but know that you can write your next new chapter. Seek out support from loved ones and friends, and do not be afraid to speak with a professional in helping you process pain and trauma.

Mind & Spirit: Your mind and intuition might feel as though they've been stuck in a bit of a fog as of late. Exercise caution when placing trust in anyone who is trying to sell you on a new spiritual program or community. While it's okay to learn as much as you can about new practices for traditions, this is not a time to see anything with rose-colored glasses. This is a time to focus on you, not to throw yourself into something new to forget your pain.

Body: Mental health issues may continue to impact your physiological health and you might find yourself feeling a bit perplexed when it comes to acquiring answers for a way forward. If your intuition has been nudging you to seek out additional advice, it might be time to do just that. Remember to take mental health symptoms seriously and seek out the appropriate provider.

Money: Your ego may be a bit fragile as of late, so don't take anything too personally. Even if others around you are condescending or behaving in a toxic way, you can choose to disengage or not. Try not to let the fragile egos of others affect your progress. You may find yourself making a lot of sacrifices when it comes to finance or your professional life, and it may not be correct to do so. You might have the inclination to place the blame on something or someone else rather than examining how you might have contributed to this situation. Take a deep breath and step back before making any risky long-term decisions.

Meditations: Do you need to let go of past hurts? Are old cycles of pain holding you back? Is it time to move on?

4 Of Swords

Overview: The Four of Swords is about seeking your inner truth. You might be experiencing being cut off or out of touch with your emotions. This is a time to take a step back regroup and reassess the situation. Look to springtime as a period for change. It's important to keep both your priorities and emotions in check. Any lingering issues causing you distress will pass. This is not a time to be paralyzed with fear, but to take a step back and allow for processing and introspection. Take time to meditate upon what you need to be happy. You can learn a lot from your dreams and intuition at this time. Four of Swords indicates that you may have some potential challenges on the horizon. Now is the time for introspection and to rejuvenate body, mind, and spirit. This is a time to go within and problem solve from a place of self-compassion and love.

Love: This indicates a need to take a step back or someone in your love life is shying away or detaching at this time. Remember that nothing is permanent, and when people need their space, whether you or the other person, sometimes this can bring the utmost clarity. However, it's important to remember that communication is key. Before taking a step back it might be ideal to express you are needs and wants as concisely as possible in order to prevent any misunderstanding before withdrawing. If you are looking for a relationship, be sure to give people their space and not force anything to happen. This is not a time to push your way into someone's heart, nor is it ideal for someone to force their way into your life. This is a time of reflection and figuring out specifically what you want in a romantic relationship and documenting it accordingly. When you tell the Universe what you want specifically, it is then that you can get your answer.

Mind & Spirit: This is the time of serious an intentional reflection and spiritual restoration. Perhaps you need to take a break from your everyday routine and distance yourself from sources of stress. The time that you take to restore your spirit and mind can have long-term benefits. This is also an indication that it might be time to seek out a professional for advice.

Body: Your health can greatly benefit from taking time for rest and relaxation. Maybe this is an ideal time to start planning a vacation, even if it's a short one, to gain some perspective.

Money: This may be an ideal time to take some time off from work or to catch up on paying off any outstanding debt. If you have any new ideas that could make you money in the long term, right now is the time to keep exciting new projects to yourself. This is a time to reflect on your overall goals in to tie up any loose ends that may prevent you from moving forward.

Travel: You may be taking a trip where the focus is rest in recuperation from a long period of stress. This should do you a lot of good and give perspective that you might have needed.

Geography: Fiji

Locations: Funeral parlors, bedrooms, or isolated venues.

4 Of Swords Reversed

Overview: The Four of Swords in reverse indicates that you might not be taking the necessary actions to improve your life. While the truth may hurt it's important to know it and understand it. You may also be experiencing difficulty in expressing yourself with your authentic voice. Four Swords in reverse indicates that you or someone you know might be doing what they can to keep themselves preoccupied to avoid making decisions or addressing conflict.

Love: You might be experiencing difficulties in your romantic relationships concerning how much time and effort either of you are putting in to make things work. Maybe you feel like you haven't been able to speak from your heart on issues that matter. This is not a time to run away from conflict, but to address it in a calm and mature way. Don't overextend yourself when it comes to love, as it may have consequences that will impact other aspects of your life. Know that right now might not be the best time for your romantic relationships but know that better connections are on the horizon, whether it's deepening a current bond or opening yourself up for something completely new. Be sure that you're open to trying new things in order to make something work, but if not, think outside the box when it comes to meeting someone new.

Mind & Spirit: This may be a time to address any blocks or issues with your energy field or chakras. Remember, you are pure consciousness. Take time to meditate and align yourself with the source. Stillness is key.

Body: You may be feeling exhausted or overtired as of late. This might be a good time to retreat and go within to figure out how you can better manage your stress in order to reduce its impact on your health.

Money: When it comes to your professional life now might be the time to take that much needed vacation. If you're looking for a new career, now might be the time to start thinking about the best ways to network in the steps that you must take in order to manifest your goals. This is a time to rethink your strategy. When it comes to finances you might be experiencing a bit of anxiety and may need to take a step back to re-evaluate your long-term objectives.

Meditations: Are you telling the truth? Is it possible that others are misleading you right now? Are you making promises that you don't intend to keep or can't keep? Are you ignoring the facts?

5 Of Swords

Overview: The Five of Swords indicates heeding the call to a quest. The number 8 is significant within this card. You may be taking a journey or embarking upon a spiritual quest. Autumn is a time where this may potentially occur. Remember that the true spiritual journey is a transformative one that will enable you to break free from karmic cycles and pain in order to align with your Higher Self. In order to reach out and grab opportunities, you must let go of the past and leave old ways of thinking and doing behind. This is a time for adventure as well as fertility. This is a time about breaking old patterns, creating new ideas, and easier paths ahead if you allow yourself to break free from the chains of yesterday. Five of Swords indicates that you might have won recent battle that could cost you in other ways. This could have been a loss of an important friendship or contact because of one's ego. Ask yourself if it's better to win and to appear to be right and be lonely or to come from a place of understanding and work on strengthening friendship.

Love: When it comes to romance be sure to watch your words, or you might regret saying something that you can never take back. Think at what cost is a current relationship or a potential partnership if you speak from a place of malice. This is not a good time to have a win-at-all-costs attitude but to come from a place of compassion. If you must express yourself from a place of authenticity and define healthy boundaries, you can do so in a diplomatic way and get the answers you're looking for. If you do it from a place of ego, you may be engaging in toxic cycles that you need to address rather than pointing the fingers outward. Ask yourself, whether you're in a relationship or looking for one, if your current attitude towards love, in both how you give and receive, aligns with your Higher Self. If not, what changes do you need to make?

Mind & Spirit: Bear in mind that the path that you're on for spiritual wellness might not be a one-size-fits-all solution for anyone else. Remember that your own path is for you and that you don't need to convince anyone to jump on board. If you find yourself in a bit of a spiritual rut, take a step back and figure out what needs you want met and figure out the way forward from there.

Body: If you're holding on to anger and resentment, know that leaving issues unresolved can have long-term effects on your health. It's important to feel safe and supported in expressing yourself, and instead of holding on to trauma or anger it's time to release and process in a healthy way.

Money: 8 is a significant number when it comes to finances or your professional endeavors. Remember that diplomacy is imperative and to take ego out of your communication. Exercise caution when it comes to finances and refrain from hasty decision-making.

Travel: You may be taking a trip to get much needed rejuvenation, and this may put distance between you and someone you care about.

Geography: North America, Vanuatu, Papua New Guinea, Solomon Islands

Locations: Arbitration offices, group therapy practices, or accident sites.

5 Of Swords Reversed

Overview: When Five of Swords is in reverse you might not be seeing things as they truly are and looking through rose-colored glasses. This is a sign to cut energy cords and to break free of childhood patterns. Instead of looking outward, you might need to look within as your own ego and insecurity may be hindering progress and blocking opportunities. You will have the chance to move on and travel down a more prosperous path, but you might require the guidance of someone else who has traveled a similar way. Five of Swords in reverse indicates that you might have come to a realization that some battles aren't worth fighting and are ready to walk away.

Love: You might be experiencing a period of reflection after going through an argument or disagreement. You may be feeling hesitant to apologize if you are in some way at fault or someone you might be dealing with might have a hard time admitting fault. Remember that it takes two to tango, so culpability will not be entirely on your side. It would be beneficial if everyone was open and honest with how they have participated in the problem in order to effectively resolve conflict. If you're looking for a relationship, you might have felt like giving up altogether. It's okay to take a step back. Re-evaluate your wants and needs in addition to deal-breakers and boundaries but be sure to be ready to communicate those needs up front. In all matters of the heart, pick your battles wisely.

Mind & Spirit: This is a time to re-evaluate spiritual needs and whether you need to take a completely different approach or path to your Higher Self. It's important to take a step back and re-evaluate what truly makes you happy.

Body: Mental health issues may be impacting your physiological health but know that taking a step back and pulling away from stressful situations might be ideal. It's okay if you can't do everything on your own. Sometimes it's best to reach out to others for help.

Money: You might have experienced multiple failed attempts to resolve a workplace or financial issue as though you've exhausted all options in words. This is an ideal time to reevaluate your long-term plans and consider a brand-new approach. This is a time to be honest about your intentions both with yourself and other people. This is not a time to let your ego get the best of you or to lose you're cool. If you do notice anything unethical happening around you, do not engage in direct conflict but report any questionable activities to the proper authorities.

Meditations: Are you holding on to old ways of thinking that no longer serve you? Are you allowing fear to hold you back? Are you seeing the whole picture of what needs to be done next?

6 Of Swords

Overview: Six of Swords is about travel in between spiritual worlds and cycles. New opportunities are about to open before us especially pertaining to spiritual development, and you might notice these changes around sunrise and sunset. You might find yourself waking up at odd hours of the night for no reason, but there is a reason. This is an invitation to align yourself with the Universe. This is a great time for both intuition and fertility. It's important to move through the cycle of grieving to awaken into a renewed sense of happiness and a new state of being. You are the source of prophecy right now. Listen to your inner voice. Six of Swords indicates potentially having to rebuild and start over. You might be experiencing loss or feelings of regret but know that some sacrifices are necessary to be happy. Focus on the new chapter ahead and what you can be grateful for in the present in order to transition into a better condition.

Love: If you're currently involved in a relationship, you might be planning or embarking upon an international trip or a permanent move abroad. This card also indicates distancing yourself from pain or a situation that is no longer ideal. Travel seems to be the greater indication of what's going to be required to gain a macro perspective of your life. It is also possible, regardless of your relationship status, that you might need to put some distance between yourself and people who do not have your best interests in mind. This is a time of major transition and planning a move that will impact your love life in the long-term. Right now, it's imperative to make bold moves, especially in the physical sense, to distance yourself from toxic relationships, friendships, or situations that are no longer healthy for you.

Mind & Spirit: You might be needing to take a journey or make a long-term move that is far from your hometown to gain greater spiritual perspective. Perhaps now it's time to put up greater boundaries, both spiritual and physical, between you and others. When you make bold moves in order to love yourself better, you'll find that the answers you've been looking for finally appear.

Body: This is a time to seek out a variety of opinions regarding your health. If your primary care provider is not giving you the answers that you need, this card indicates that you might need to see a specialist. This might also involve long-distance travel in order to find answers or to give yourself a break from your immediate surroundings which may be a primary source of pain.

Money: Two is a significant number. You may be considering accepting a new position that requires long distance travel or living abroad. In any case, this indicates a major change and how you deal with finances or where you work. This is a time to also diversify your income streams and not to take any risky gambles. Major changes should produce major rewards.

Travel: This is a great time for movement especially concerning international travel or relocation.

Geography: Greece, Arizona, New Mexico, Australia

Locations: Rivers, bodies of water, airports, harbors, nautical or air travel.

6 Of Swords Reversed

Overview: The Six of Swords in reverse indicates that you might be hanging on to something that no longer benefits you. It's important to take time to mourn but it's also important to release the past instead of getting locked into harmful cycles. Plans that you have in motion at this time may not manifest and are likely to experience delays. This is a time to rethink and reassess. Six of Swords in reverse indicates that you might be unwilling to accept a change due to clinging to the past. This might leave you unprepared and unequipped to take on challenges.

Love: You might be finding that a recent change in your love life is difficult to process. You might be feeling like you're stuck in a bit of a romantic rut and that your situation is a bit undesirable. This is not a time to cling to negative thought patterns or the past. No matter how much you've given in to a situation, if it's been unhealthy for you then it's time to re-evaluate your priorities and think about letting go if needed. This is a time where effective communication is key in order to resolve problems rather than a combative stance. Overall, this is a time to leave your comfort zone in order to make drastic changes that will involve long-distance travel.

Mind & Spirit: This is a time to address your spiritual life from a place of love and compassion. Perhaps it is time to let go of outdated ways of thinking in order to clear your path and move forward. If you feel like you've been stuck in a bit of a rut, then it's important to figure out what changes need to be made and act accordingly.

Body: You might be holding on too tightly to the way that you've been handling your physiological health. Perhaps it fuels a bit scary to make major changes to your diet, exercise, and nutrition regimen. However, you need to keep your long-term health goals in mind and make decisions better for your benefit rather than deciding from a place of fear.

Money: You might be experiencing delays in travel plans when it comes to your profession or your finances. Especially in journeys over large bodies of water, you might be hearing news of weather causing the delays which may drastically change your plans altogether. This is a time to be meticulous and detail-oriented when it comes to any official documents or important official correspondence. This is a time to think about what you can do to diversify your income streams in order to be successful as an independent person. When it comes to finances in general, this may indicate some frustration in achieving your goals. However, it also means that your ability to become independent is even more likely than it ever has been. Be careful with potential new partnerships or lending your trust with anyone new. This is not a time to gamble but to make smart money moves.

Meditations: Have you examined every possible opportunity and outcome? Are you being impatient? Are you not seeing patterns being repeated and how harmful they can be? Are you afraid of seeking spiritual guidance?

7 Of Swords

Overview: Seven of Swords is about the proper use of one's knowledge. This is a time of increased intuition and spiritual knowledge as it pertains to the occult and metaphysical world. You need to be careful about keeping confidential information to yourself and having alternative plans in case things don't go our way. This is a card of intelligence, keen observation, and using your magic appropriately. You might be having trouble and obtaining knowledge that you want in order to manifest your goals. However, you can expect new visions, new messages from the Universe, and tapping into your inner magic. Use your powers wisely. Seven of Swords indicates a person around you might be trying to deceive you or violate your boundaries. If you are attempting to deceive or take advantage of someone, think twice because your likelihood of getting caught is quite high. Act with integrity, and if something is gnawing at your psyche, pay attention to it.

Love: This is a time to be observant in your love life. Whether you're in a committed relationship or single, this is a time to be vigilant in matters of the heart especially when it comes to any red flags that nudge at your intuition. If you're trying to deceive someone, or if someone is trying to deceive you, proceed with caution an act with integrity. This is a time for open and honest communication rather than beating around the bush and allowing ego to manifest and cause even more problems. If you're currently looking for a relationship, be sure that you're not projecting a facade of disinterest or not being your authentic self. Show up as who you are and be clear about your relationship goals and boundaries.

Mind & Spirit: This is a time to be cautious of anyone who could potentially take advantage of you when it comes to spiritual Wellness. Remember that you don't need to pay to play on the path to your Higher Self. Exercise extreme caution when it comes to anyone trying to convert you to a new belief system.

Body: Be vigilant about your health and different ways you can achieve your overall wellness goals. Be sure to seek out the proper professional guidance and not take passing advice too seriously especially when it comes to people who are not qualified to give it.

Money: This is a time to be highly vigilant when it comes to matters of finance and your professional life as someone may be trying to deceive you. Be on guard about people trying to collect intelligence on money matters or your career. This is also a time to not be complacent when it comes to your profession. It's important to act with integrity in the workplace as well as your personal finances. You might also be dealing worth intellectual or financial theft which needs to be dealt with in a timely manner. Remember it is important to act with integrity.

Travel: Be careful in accepting some any offers that require travel or you may find yourself deceived.

Geography: Australia

Locations: Attorney offices, courts for civil suits, amusement parks, or factories.

7 Of Swords Reversed

Overview: When Seven of Swords is in reverse you might be dabbling in spiritual realms in which you should not. You should also take care not to let your pride interfere with your endeavors or in obtaining new knowledge. Dipping your toes into the spirit world might not have the impact you think it will. Beware of misusing any psychic powers or occult abilities. You may be experiencing or partaking in psychic spying. Seven of Swords in reverse indicates that you're having a difficult time moving forward due to feeling overwhelmed or encumbered by life circumstances. Ask yourself if there's anything that you're doing right now, whether it's personal habits or fears, that might be keeping you from manifesting your dreams.

Love: You might not be completely honest about your intentions when it comes to your love life. Perhaps you're clinging to outdated modes of thinking that are keeping you from experiencing your ideal romantic life. Integrity is key on all sides, and it's important to speak from a place of authenticity and be sure that you're receiving the same in return. You might also be experiencing feelings of frustration or disappointment with your love life. Think about a variety of ways romantic conflicts can be solved, especially when they allow an open and safe space for everyone to express their concerns and needs without judgment. Remember that every party in a romantic relationship deserves the dignity of honest communication. If you've been experiencing infidelity, this is a time for full accountability that is fair to everyone. This is not a time to take relationship shortcuts or to engage in questionable behavior behind someone's back.

Mind & Spirit: This is a great time to go within and trust your intuition when it comes to your needs and what you should do next regarding your spiritual path.

Body: Now is the time to consider taking a needed long-term break in order to give your body in mind a chance to recuperate from a period of stress.

Money: You may be experiencing difficulties when it comes to feeling appreciated at work. Perhaps you feel that you've been under a microscope lately. Be sure that you are acting with integrity and that no one will have any reason to pin any blame on you. This is a time to communicate in a way that is open and honest in order to build upon trust when it comes to matters of finance or your profession. If you're thinking about changing jobs or if you feel like your position is at risk, now is the time to be honest with yourself about your long-term plans and needs. Seek out the advice of a trusted professional before making any major decisions.

Meditations: Are you misusing your skills or knowledge? Are you being discreet in information?

8 Of Swords

Overview: Eight of Swords indicates that it is time to free yourself from strong emotion. There is a great shift of intense emotion around you at this time. However, you will have the opportunity to express yourself in a variety of creative ways. You must take care not to let your emotions get the best of you. Worries or anxieties may be blocking your inner voice an ability to see clearly. This is the time to seek out guidance. If you don't address your emotional issues at this time, you're likely to impede your own movement. Break free of the past and get some fresh air. Eight of Swords indicates being caught up in self-limiting beliefs. This is an indication that you have the power to break free from your situation, and the main person who is holding you back is you. This is a time to reclaim your power by shifting your perspective. Sure, there are challenges before you, however, you the power to overcome.

Love: You may be experiencing an overwhelming feeling of helplessness or a victim mentality when it comes to your romantic life. This appears to be more of a matter of limitations that you've placed on yourself or a general fear of major changes that might be necessary. Even if you are experiencing any sense of discontent, ask yourself if staying put is also somewhat of a comfort zone. Also, you might want to ask what you have to gain from loving yourself better. In any case, you might be feeling trapped by your circumstances. However, much of this comes from your own thinking. You have a lot more power to change your situation than you're giving yourself credit for. If you're choosing to stay in a relationship that has surpassed its expiration date, then it's time to re-evaluate your boundaries and needs. Is it better to be stuck in a bad situation? Or to be open to a wonderful new chapter? Remember that the person who will show up in your life to change it for the better will always be you.

Mind & Spirit: You may have placed unfair limitations on yourself when it comes to achieving your spiritual goals. Remember that the only person holding you back is you at this time and it's important to let go of your fears in order to embrace something new exciting and positive. Change is not as scary as you think it is.

Body: It appears that negative thinking can have an impact on your physiological health. Seek out the appropriate professional guidance.

Money: You may be feeling stuck in a professional or financial rut and are feeling powerless to change it. However, many other opportunities to improve your situation are within your reach if you are courageous enough to take the blinders of your comfort zone off. In order to reap great rewards, you must be willing to put yourself out there in a new brave way. When it comes to finances, you also have a lot more power than you realize to diversify your income. Think positively.

Travel: You may turn down travel or a potential opportunity out of fear.

Geography: Australia

Locations: Places that are abundant in pine trees, prisons, or asylums.

8 Of Swords Reversed

Overview: When Eight of Swords is in reverse you may be airing out your emotions in the wrong crowd or the wrong time or oversharing when you shouldn't. This is not a time to talk but to take direct action. There will be opportunities that will present themselves to you, but you need to keep it to yourself. This is time to let go of the past so that you can be fully present and prepared for the future. Eight of Swords in reverse indicates that a difficult time in your life is ending. After all the lessons have been learned, you can move on to a better chapter and will have the tools and knowledge of how to avoid similar situations and succeed.

Love: You are in a position where you are finally ready to take back your personal power and speak with your authentic voice. It appears that something has recently taking place that shook you awake and has you looking at your situation differently. You are ready to get to the bottom of issues in your romantic life whether it's an existing relationship or if you're thinking of pursuing new romantic partnerships. In any case, this is a major indicator to focus on loving yourself first before providing for anyone else. Remember that you cannot pour from an empty cup and that you can attract greater love when you've given that love to yourself first.

Mind & Spirit: You may feel a new burst of energy and a sense of calm when it comes to your spiritual mindset. This is a time to tend to old wounds in order to process and heal. This is a great time to adjust your priorities in to allow for true and lasting growth. Many obstacles you have faced and overcome have prepared you for a bright new chapter ahead. You might also find that your story may be beneficial to someone else who is trying to process trauma. Sometimes when we share our narrative of growth after trauma, it can be somewhat of a road map to someone else who is struggling and not that far along on their journey.

Body: This is a time to listen to what your body is telling you and to follow through on seeking medical advice as appropriate. This is not a time to manage health issues on your own but to seek guidance from an expert.

Money: If you're looking to make major changes when it comes to your profession or finances, know that this is an optimal time for opening yourself up to a positive new chapter. This is an ideal time to focus on long-term financial rewards, especially as it pertains to retirement or emergency funds. Professional opportunities may come from unexpected places, so keep an open mind.

Meditations: Have you been repeating old patterns? Are you refusing to resolve old issues? Are you playing out events in your head without doing anything about it?

9 Of Swords

Overview: The Nine of Swords indicates finding answers in dreams. This is a time to pay attention to the dream world. Dreams will become more colorful and possibly even more lucid than normal. Through dreams you can gain insight into problems and circumstances going on around you. Remember that sometimes we lose things that are no longer healthy for us. This is not a time to compromise your goals and dreams. The only thing that's stopping your progress is compromise. When you deal with the past and process those memories accordingly, you can open new doors to happiness and success. Nine of Swords indicates that you might be consumed by your own thoughts in dealing with an increase of anxiety and fear. Be careful of manifesting negative energy and thoughts into reality.

Love: This is the time to go within and meditate regarding issues with your romantic life. This is not a time to ignore your intuition, especially when it has to do with unhealthy relationship patterns. Romantic issues might be plaguing your psyche at this time, and you may notice vivid and even troubling dreams hinting at problems in your waking life. This is an indication that you will need to start confronting all the red flags in your life and to be proactive in handling issues of possible deception or infidelity. However, before tackling any issues, be sure that you've spent time talking about it with a trusted professional or journaling about it to gain some perspective. If you're not in a relationship, this indicates needing to address any worries or anxieties pertaining to a starting anything new. If you don't take the steps to resolve unhealed trauma it will carry over into your next relationship.

Mind & Spirit: You might have had difficulties getting a good night's rest, especially after intense dreams maybe haunting you at night. This is a time to stand up, be brave, and face your fears. There is no sense in allowing worry to take control of your life. Decide on a course of action and proceed.

Body: Anxiety and repressed trauma may be impacting your physical health. This is also not a time to turn to substances to numb the pain. It's important to address trauma or any unhealed wounds with a professional.

Money: Stress about your career or personal finances will do you no good so long as you do nothing. Remember that no one is an island and if someone is offering help or a new opportunity, be open to change. This is not a time for risky financial behavior or questionable decisions. If you're unhappy with your current circumstances, ask for help.

Travel: You may be highly anxious about taking a long-distance trip. Consider all your options and ask yourself whether it's fear holding you back or if you have real causes for concern.

Geography: Australia

Locations: Asylums, battlefields, or theaters.

9 Of Swords Reversed

Overview: When Nine of Swords is in reverse, you might be having an issue with distinguishing fantasy from reality. Don't rely on dreams to carry you through, you have to act as well. You might not be letting go of the past as you may need to and wallowing in sorrow and pity. This is the time to wake up an act on your goals no matter how difficult the path ahead may seem. Nine of swords in reverse indicates that you might be overreacting for no reason. This is a time to focus your energy on being present and not looking at the past too much or fretting about the future.

Love: You may be ignoring your authentic voice or intuition when it comes to your love life. You might be keeping up a façade that you're happy, but deep down you know that there are real issues that you must address in real time. Perhaps you are holding on to irrational fears, but you must get to the bottom of what's hurting you. This is a time of great courage in order to make positive changes. Expressing yourself will provide a sense of liberation, so perhaps it's time to reach out for professional help in order to do effective shadow work and break free from toxic relationship cycles. If you're looking to start a new relationship, take things slow and be sure to be honest about your intentions, boundaries, and needs.

Mind & Spirit: Holding onto negative thought patterns may be obstructing your spiritual path. This is an important time to face your nightmares or anything else that's keeping you up at night. Try documenting your thoughts and feelings in a journal in order to gain a new perspective on how you might want to proceed.

Body: This is a time to be proactive when it comes to your health especially concerning self-destructive behavior. There are issues regarding your health that should not be put off any longer. Seek the appropriate medical advice.

Money: This is a time to be extra cautious when signing any official documents or starting any new business partnerships. Examine all pros and cons before moving forward. If you feel that your work is unappreciated or someone is taking the spotlight away from you after all your efforts manifested positive results, think about different ways to change your circumstances. When it comes to money and investments, exercise extreme caution in placing your trust in anyone to handle your finances. If something doesn't feel right, trust your intuition.

Meditations: Are you viewing life with rose-colored glasses? Are you hanging on to the past or cycles of behavior that no longer benefit you? Are you ignoring your dreams? Are you being realistic?

10 Of Swords

Overview: Ten of Swords indicates cycles pertaining to destruction but also resurrection. This is a card that indicates rock bottom. This is a powerful time for rebirth and starting anew. Remember that we sometimes lose things in order for new opportunities to come our way. It is important now more than ever to maintain a sense of humor in life. During times of trouble and trauma it's important to have healthy coping mechanisms. Right now, things might not be the way they seem. Think of this instance like that of a phoenix, the legendary bird that rises from its own ashes. Remember that rebirth is possible. Ten of Swords indicates rock bottom and potential betrayal. This card of course is a heavy one, but it's also indicative of the worst being over. Sometimes when things end or chapters come to a close it can be painful, but you will soon have the means to carry on and overcome.

Love: Whether you're in a relationship or looking for one, you may feel as though your romantic life has hit rock bottom. This is a time for honest self-evaluation and how you might take the appropriate steps to improve your romantic life and to break free of toxic relationship cycles as well as karmic relationships. Be careful of dealing with deceptive people who do not have your best interests at heart.

Mind & Spirit: When it comes to your spiritual life, you may be reassessing what's working for you and what's not. This is a time of drastic change. Perhaps those who have assisted you on your spiritual path may have been discovered to be untrustworthy. While you may be feeling a significant amount of pain, remember that from here the only way is up. Release regrets and forgive yourself.

Body: Seek out trusted medical advice when it comes to your health and be proactive about dealing with problems immediately.

Money: Pay attention to blue and green logos or signs when it comes to business partnerships or financial opportunities. Proceed with caution. Opportunities may be coming to a painful end. This is not a time to make any risky financial decisions or to place your trust in people who may be out to deceive you. This is a time for a logical and strategic reevaluation of your finances.

Travel: This is not an ideal time for travel. Consider all your options and plans but proceed with caution if travel is necessary.

Geography: Egypt, Australia

Locations: Operating room, dental office, acupuncture office, ancient ruins, or landfills.

10 Of Swords Reversed

Overview: When Ten of Swords in reverse you might not be looking at circumstances with the proper perspective. You might feel that there's a shadow lingering above you and that it's hard to see the future in a positive way. However, this is a time to focus on new and upcoming possibilities. People you might have depended on before might not be available to you right now. This is a time to become more present and to tune into your inner voice. Ten of Swords in reverse also indicates a potential negative mindset and letting fear override your better judgment. This also indicates that a lack of trust may prevent it you from experiencing true happiness. Remember that when you focus on the negative or your fears, you're projecting that into the Universe, and it will continue to manifest it. If you want to be happy you must ask yourself honestly, what does that look like?

Love: If you're proactive about your love life and healing past trauma, then the only way from here is up. Perhaps you've been experiencing retraumatization or a recent event that has caused great distress. However, there appears to be a light at the end of the tunnel. This is about not accepting unhealthy circumstances, whether you're in a relationship or looking for one. This is about a fresh new start, and while things may be a bit alarming or even uncomfortable at times, know that if you are taking the appropriate steps to love yourself better and enforce healthy boundaries then you're on the right path.

Mind & Spirit: This is not a time to cling to negative thought patterns but a wonderful time for a brand-new clean slate when it comes to your spiritual path. Think about your spiritual needs and what you need to achieve a sense of inner peace. This is also a time of relief after a long period of stress.

Body: You may feel as though you've gained new perspective regarding your health, and the path forward might seem a lot clearer than it ever has been. This is a time to be proactive when it comes to healing any physiological issues. Remember that you are your best advocate.

Money: You may have been experiencing major changes with your career or an end to a business partnership. Now is the time to reflect on the best strategy for moving forward and what it may take for you to reach your financial goals as well as your professional goals. This is not a time to revert to negative or destructive thought patterns that hold you back.

Meditations: Are your emotions clouding your judgment right now? Are you failing to act on new opportunities out of fear? Is it time to get spiritual guidance?

Page Of Swords

Overview: Page of Swords indicates new messages, high energy, and even magic. This is a time of alchemy, so watch out for new opportunities coming your way and remember to channel your own inner magic. Do not let your guard down at this time. Using your voice an effective communication will be of the utmost importance very soon. Exercise that voice to get what you want in need. Right now, you might be more successful collaborating or working with the group then going it alone. This is a time of developing your creativity and magical power. Remember there are opportunities all around you. Page of Swords indicates you or someone who has found their stride. This is also an indication of increased energy and communication. This might also foretell a new journey is coming up soon.

Love: Messages regarding love will be important at this time. Perhaps it's an email, a text, or some kind of correspondence that will provide some insight into your romantic life. Pay attention to the way your loved one or a potential partner is behaving. Is their body language corresponding with the words that they speak? This is a time of fun yet open and honest communication. If you're trying to get to the bottom of an unresolved issue in a current romantic relationship, think about different ways to make everyone feel comfortable in expressing themselves honestly. You might also receive a message that provides you an answer that you've been waiting for, but also be prepared to give people their space. There's nothing wrong with getting out there and getting to know new people - just try to have a little fun in the process.

Mind & Spirit: This is not a time to be aggressive with others or yourself regarding your spiritual path. Keep an open mind and trust in your intuition.

Body: This is not a time to push your body too hard or overextend yourself physically in any way. If you're looking to get out stress through physical exercise, be sure that you're doing it in a way that is safe.

Money: When it comes to making any financial decisions now is not the time to take shortcuts. You may not have all the knowledge that you need to proceed in investments, and it might be beneficial to seek out the guidance of an expert who could help guide your decisions. If you're currently employed, you might be facing difficulties in the workplace that stem from miscommunication. Act with integrity and humility in all matters of professional correspondence, But don't be self-deprecating.

Travel: Be careful of overextending yourself when it comes to travel or not knowing as much as you need to before you leave.

Geography: Australia

Locations: Electronics stores, café's where people work remotely, sports arenas, or children's hospitals.

Page Of Swords Reversed

Overview: When Page of Swords is in reverse this indicates that you may be having difficulties in taking advantage of opportunities. Be watchful of the people around you as they might be taking advantage of you. Any plans or endeavors that you have in the works right now may be delayed. However, you might be surprised to find that plans will manifest in strange new unexpected ways. It's important to look closely and exercise situational awareness of what may be going on around you especially if something doesn't feel quite right. You may be experiencing difficulty in communicating and may experience misunderstandings. Stay away from gossip or people that engage in it. Page of Swords in reverse also indicates someone who is all talk and no action. Someone who says that they are *ride or die*, but it's a lot of die and no ride. This is potentially you or someone who is jumping into a situation too quickly without thinking everything through, and in doing so might prove to be a colossal waste of time and energy.

Love: Be cautious when it comes to miscommunications in love. You or your partner, or a potential partner, might have difficulty in processing honest communication. Perhaps the truth is hurting someone right now. Just be cautious in the way that you communicate with others, especially when it comes to any electronic correspondence. Someone might be feeling a bit nervous in communicating wants, needs, or underlying issues. This is a time to summon the courage to speak with your authentic voice and communicate what you need to love and to feel loved. You might be dealing with someone who is not telling you the truth or concealing parts of the truth for their benefit. Be careful of speaking out or acting out without thinking. Once you release words into the Universe, you will not be able to take them back. There is also a possibility that messages are missed altogether.

Mind & Spirit: Be careful of surrounding yourself with people who engage in gossip or violate your boundaries to the point where it's affecting your spiritual life. Deal with problems openly and honestly and consider what it's going to take for you to be happy.

Body: You might need to get a second opinion when it comes to your health. Do not disclose any information to others outside of medical providers pertaining to your overall wellness. Be proactive and don't discuss any health concerns with others, or you might find that it becomes a topic of conversation when you're not around.

Money: Exercise additional caution when it comes to miscommunication in professional endeavors or managing your finances. You might also be receiving news that leaves you feeling a bit disappointed when it comes to a business partnership or another professional opportunity. But do not despair, other opportunities are on the way.

Meditations: Are you sharing secrets or information with other people in order to gain friendships? Are you speaking maliciously about others in order to be liked? Is someone potentially spreading unsavory gossip about you in order to gain social status or a financial opportunity?

Knight Of Swords

Overview: The Knight of Swords indicates protection in our plans and endeavors. You might experience changes in the form of 7s or 10s, whether it's days, weeks, or months. Right now, you are being protected, but you are also asked to trust your own intuition. This is a time to act swiftly and move without fear. You have protection on your journey ahead so now is the time to move forward and powered. Knight of Swords indicates someone who is enthusiastic and moves quickly. This may also indicate a new job or a new journey to success. This might also indicate a new endeavor that will motivate you and inspire an increase of energy. However, it's important not to take any shortcuts in any of your current projects or else it could result in long-term difficulties. If you've been awaiting news pertaining to travel, you're likely to receive a message quite soon.

Love: A burst of lively energy is indicated in your romantic life whether you're committed or looking for love. Current relationships have the potential of improved intimacy and open communication in a radical new way. If you're currently looking for a relationship you are likely to encounter someone who is quick witted, honest, and full of energy. This person can also be a bit stubborn and highly assertive with their opinion. They are passionate about their ideas and goals but can be a bit crass at times. In any case, this is about an exciting new energy in your romantic life.

Mind & Spirit: This is a great time to go within, meditate, and be ready to receive answers. This is a time of new energy and channeling this positive burst into wonderful spiritual answers.

Body: Issues pertaining to legs or vision might be cause for concern. You might be experiencing an uptick in energy and a newfound curiosity of ways to improve your overall health.

Money: ¾ is an important figure as well as 7s or 10s when it comes to new financial or business opportunities. You might notice an uptick in energy when it comes to your professional life as well as your financial gains. However, this is a time to save instead of spending it all in one go. Your motivation and drive may cause you to outshine others but have some humility about it.

Travel: You may be taking a trip that is both exciting and informative where you will meet someone who will help you expand your horizons.

Geography: New Zealand

Locations: Social events, networking opportunities, or education summits.

Knight Of Swords Reversed

Overview: When the Knight of Swords is in reverse, it indicates that there may be complications in our plans at this time. If you have long-term plans, this indicates that the first year might be the most difficult and you should do your best to be aware and prepare for any potential problems. Your plans might not be as secure as you once thought. You might find yourself wrongly accused of doing something that others were responsible for. If this is happening to you, be patient stick take a step back and observe as the truth will eventually come to light. Knight of Swords in reverse indicates being somewhat of a scatterbrain and not focusing in areas that you should. This could also indicate a person who is highly motivated and has a lot of energy but no follow through.

Love: You might be dealing with someone flighty when it comes to matters of the heart. This is not a time to look at your romantic life in a superficial way. If you're currently in a relationship, ask yourself whether you're communicating your needs or crossing boundaries. Sometimes people need a bit space and it's important not to take that personally. If you're looking for a relationship, it's important to keep an open mind and not to be too judgmental with perspective new partners.

Mind & Spirit: This is the time to reevaluate your communications with others regarding your spiritual life. This is a time to go within rather than rely on the thoughts and opinions of others.

Body: While you might not be getting all the answers that you feel that you need to understand what's going on with your physical health. Be sure to explore your options with a medical professional or find a way to see a specialist.

Money: Exercise caution when it comes to your finances and beware of overspending. This is also a warning not to place your trust in people who are presenting any get-rich-quick schemes. If it sounds too good to be true it probably is. When it comes to professional endeavors, be sure that you are acting with integrity and documenting everything appropriately. Safely guard your ideas and projects so that others do not take them from you. Be careful with any electronic correspondence that may leak vital information. Do not talk about your goals until after they've happened.

Meditations: Are you preparing as much as you should? Are you being too aggressive in your plans?

Queen Of Swords

Overview: The Queen of Swords indicate a strong spiritual perception and visions of the future. The Queen of Swords is intelligent, courageous, and highly perceptive. This is a card of messages especially pertaining to spiritual visions as your intuition is heightening more than ever. Trust in your vision and intuition no matter how strange it might seem and seek out the guidance of other spiritual practitioners as needed. This is also a great time for expressing yourself creatively especially when it comes to visions that pertain to the arts. This is the time to exercise excellent communication as it will help as manifest our vision and creative goals. Queen of Swords indicates someone who is independent and confident in their intellect. This could also be someone in your life who could be an important mentor or advisor, especially when it comes to learning a new skill or taking part in a course. This card also indicates needing to make objective decisions in taking emotion out of the picture in order to make the best logical decision.

Love: Be assertive and honest in your love life but also bear in mind everyone's boundaries. This is not a time to try to push things to happen when it comes to relationships, whether you're single or currently in a relationship. You or a romantic interest might have a sharp intellect and a highly independent streak. You might have gained great wisdom after a variety of difficulties in your romantic life. However, be cautious with your words while speaking with your authentic voice. It's important to be honest but it's also important to be compassionate. If you're currently looking for love, be careful not to be too impulsive.

Mind & Spirit: Getting in touch with your feelings might be ideal at this time instead of overanalyzing your spiritual path and purpose. Your intuition will be especially sharp now so pay attention to visions, dreams, and messages from the Universe.

Body: Focusing on stress management may be ideal at this time to improve your overall health.

Money: When it comes to your professional endeavors or business opportunities, be sure that you are not telling everyone your plans. This is a time to guard information and keep your cards close to your chest if you expect to manifest your goals. This is also a time to not engage in any unnecessary professional drama nor is at a time to react to any ego bruising. You may benefit from seeking out the guidance of a wise professional who has an abundance of advice. Be open to seeking alternate routes on the path to your success.

Travel: You may be taking a trip in which you will be seeking new skills and information to realize a creative goal.

Geography: Brazil (Amazon), Mexico, Central America, South America, New Zealand

Locations: Creative entrepreneurship conferences, technologically innovative expos, theaters, or bookshops.

Queen Of Swords Reversed

Overview: The Queen of Swords in reverse indicates low emotional development or regulation. Your own emotions may be coloring your perceptions, or you may be perceiving things the way that you want to and not how things are. You may need to get a bit of sunshine or play with some paint on canvas. Queen of Swords in reverse indicates someone who might be judgmental, cold, and somewhat of a bully. If you or someone you know is allowing their ego to take the wheel, they risk their reputation as a result.

Love: You might have a skewed perception when it comes to your romantic life. In matters of communication, whether in a relationship or embarking upon a new one, it's important to not jump to conclusions or to act from an insecure place. Be open to hearing the perspectives of a loved one or a potential partner. Try to keep an open mind and an open heart. You or someone you love might be feeling tremendously misunderstood at this time.

Mind & Spirit: There might be somebody you're dealing with regarding your spiritual path who was once helpful but is seemingly taking a harsh approach that is leaving you to question whether or not their advice should be taken into consideration. People might not mean what they say at this time and it's important not to take any harsh words too personally. Reevaluate your situation and figure out what it is that you need at this time to feel like your best self.

Body: Health issues may be emotionally related. Monitor vitamin intake.

Money: Someone may be trying to block your progress or stand in the way of you achieving a goal, whether it's financial or professional. It may feel as though you're experiencing unnecessary delays on your path to success. Be sure it's not you standing in your own way either. Get all the information that you can before making any professional or financial changes in your life. This is a time to be extra careful when it comes to any correspondence relating to your finances. Double check your accounts, payments, or any documents pertaining to your overall financial wellness. Mistakes can be made at this time, but if you're careful you can prevent financial loss.

Meditations: Is your perception contributing to gossip? Are you abusing your spiritual visions? Are you being misunderstood?

King Of Swords

Overview: The King of Swords is a card of assertive leadership and guidance. This is a sign to also assert your own leadership and guidance as needed, to become your own authority and take charge. People around you might find you more reliable and patient. You might find that others may be changing their opinions about you for the better. Now is the time to move forward aggressively toward your goals. You know what's best for you so follow your own inner voice rather than the voice of others. King of Swords represents someone who is highly intelligent, a gifted communicator, and has a clear vision for success. This may also be a mentor type figure who you could trust and who could provide reliable information.

Love: When it comes to matters of the heart it's important to think and act with your authentic voice. If you're currently in a relationship, this is a reminder to be fair and objective when it comes to making any decisions. It's important to use both your heart and mind to make the right decision. The person that you're dealing with could also be someone who is an excellent communicator but might also seem emotionally distant. If you're currently looking for a relationship, you might encounter someone who is very intelligent who you can share lively conversations with but may not always show up romantically in ways that you desire. You might also be seeking the advice of a third party to lend their observations before making any decisions regarding your romantic life. While you don't want to conform to other people's expectations, it might also be important to try to look at things from an objective standpoint.

Mind & Spirit: Now is the time to work on connecting with your Higher Self and trusting your authentic voice. This is a time to also look for new creative ways to open up and broaden your spiritual horizons.

Body: You would benefit from educating yourself as best as you can regarding ways to improve your overall physical health. If you're looking for answers, it may take a while through multiple strategies to figure out the right path for you.

Money: This is a time to be proactive with your finances and resolving any outstanding issues. This is a time for humility when it comes to money and to get help is needed. In your professional life you might be encountering difficult people who are causing more stress than they are helping. However, you might come across someone who could be helpful in achieving a goal but are difficult to deal with on an interpersonal level.

Travel: You may be taking a trip where you meet someone who is highly opinionated and somewhat distant but may help you in achieving a goal.

Geography: New Zealand

Locations: IT companies, consulting firms, or embassies.

King Of Swords Reversed

Overview: King of Swords in reverse indicates that you might be trying to be a Jack-of-all-trades, master of none instead of harnessing your energy to focus on specific skills. Also, this may indicate that there might be too much structure or authority in your life. You might be too critical or strict with others, so beware of potential bullying. You may also be engaged in a traditional lifestyle that is no longer benefiting you or taking too much of an alternate approach that is not making a positive impact. King of Swords in reverse indicates someone who might be manipulative or somewhat of a bully. Be careful of people who are quick to use sharp words or who are condescending to you. You don't have to put up with reckless aggression.

Love: You may be dealing with someone who is difficult to engage with on an interpersonal level whether you are in a committed relationship or dealing with a potential new partnership. Think about if this is what you want in a long-term relationship. If not, this is a time to be open and honest about it and then act accordingly. No matter how much you love someone, it's not advisable to stick around any situation that is abusive or leaves you feeling unloved. This is the time to exercise healthy boundaries and speak with your authentic voice. You may also be dealing with someone who is a potential narcissist.

Mind & Spirit: Be careful of people who are very charismatic and assertive in their communication but are also not the most trustworthy. If your intuition is hinting that something might be wrong, you might want to pay attention. Remember that you do not need to lose yourself or your money on the path to your Higher Self.

Body: It's important to keep medical records organized and close in order to properly document what might be going on with your health. You might be dealing with someone who is not open to hearing your health concerns and you may benefit from seeking professional help from someone you feel comfortable speaking to about any current issues.

Money: You may have to compromise when it comes to your financial or professional goals. You might also be encountering someone who is quite difficult to deal with and imbalanced with their own masculine and feminine energies that is being channeled in toxic ways. This is a time to assert your professional boundaries and let your voice be known if something is happening that doesn't sit well with you. This is also a time to ask for help if needed when it comes to managing your finances or reexamining a budget.

Meditations: Are you trying to be too aggressive or rigid with others? Are you trying to compete with others? Are you overdoing any of your responses?

WANDS

Ace Of Wands

Overview: Ace of Wands is a card of action and new beginnings. It is also associated with healing, fertility, or even the pregnancy of someone close to us. This is the best time to initiate new endeavors especially when it's pertaining to your career or way of life. This is a time of maturity and transformation and to be keenly attuned to your inner voice. New opportunities are heading your way along with the awakening of unique and creative powers. Ace of Wands indicates that opportunities for success are close by. New beginnings are ahead and trust in the process.

Love: This is a time of new and exciting opportunities for your love life, whether you're in a relationship or currently looking for one. If you're currently in a relationship, you may be going through a transformative period where intimacy will be improved, and energy will increase. If you're on the lookout for a new romantic partnership, this is a great time to get out and meet someone new. Someone who is high energy and positive seems to be heading your way. This is a time of great passion and vitality. However, be careful when it comes to fertility issues as this is a time of new conception, literally or figuratively.

Mind & Spirit: You may be feeling quite optimistic regarding your spiritual life at this time. This is the time of nurturing new ideas and welcoming a sudden burst of creative energy that will have a lasting impact on your life. This is a time to make bold new moves to heighten your spiritual development.

Body: You might feel a newfound energy that is leading you to make bold new changes to improve your health. This is a great time to start a new fitness or wellness regimen. Anything that you do now will likely have long-term benefits.

Money: This is a great time to embark upon new financial and professional endeavors. New opportunities seem to be coming your way that will reinvigorate your career and creativity. This is also indicative of a financial increase from an unexpected source. This is a great card when it comes to achieving goals in manifesting dreams.

Travel: You will take a trip where new creative projects will begin to take off. Embrace this new burst of energy and it will be sure to go a long way.

Geography: Egypt, Brazil, Hawaii, Jamaica, Scandinavia, North Asia, Micronesia

Locations: Creative consulting firms, alternative fitness studios, 24/7 venues, or highways.

Ace Of Wands Reversed

Overview: The Ace of Wands in reverse indicates that you may be staying in stagnant circumstances. This is time to take a serious look at your present condition before embarking upon anything new. Do your best to plan as much as possible before committing to any new beginnings. It is also okay to delay or cancel your plans temporarily. This is a time when going it alone would be more beneficial than a collaboration. Ace of Wands in reverse indicates that there is an obstacle in your way or that your journey feels a bit off balance due to many worries, responsibilities, or complications.

Love: Whether you're in a committed relationship or looking for one, this is a time to pay extra attention in how you speak and send messages as misunderstandings may arise. This is also a sign of new conception – so be wary of fertility, whether figurative or literal.

Mind & Spirit: You might be feeling as though you're stuck in a spiritual rut, which may be resolved with setting time aside to meditate and reflect on your needs.

Body: Exercise good judgment when it comes to food, alcohol, or anything that could be done in excess. Poor decisions may lead to long-term health repercussions, so seek out guidance as needed.

Money: You may be experiencing setbacks within your finances or professional life. You may not be feeling fulfilled by your current profession and may benefit from seeking out guidance in deciding upon a new way or path forward. There seems to be an overall imbalance when it comes to your career where you may feel a sense of accomplishment in one aspect but experience interpersonal difficulties in the workplace. This is not a time to take financial risks or to be too trusting in anyone handling your accounts.

Meditations: Are you ignoring new opportunities? Are you resisting change? Are you allowing your emotions too much control over your life?

2 Of Wands

Overview: The Two of wands indicates that progress in creative endeavors will become much smoother and you will encounter a lot less resistance in the process. Your goals will be actualized. Your perseverance will be rewarded as the worst is over, so long as you maintain courage and patience. New dimensions are opening before you so trust in your inner voice and your path. Two of Wands indicates that an idea has been set in motion and that you have the power to manifest your goals. This is also an indicator of a potentially life-changing trip or journey. This is a sign for you to prepare to step out of your comfort zone and embark upon a journey that will transform your life for the better.

Love: You're currently filled with a creative force that emanates from within that has led you to a crossroad in life. This is a time to reflect on your past relationships and appreciate how far you've come on your romantic journey. You have the power to manifest the love life you want if you simply believe in yourself. It's important to achieve a sense of balance within, and then reflect that in your partnerships. If you're currently in a relationship, this is a great time to think about what balance means and your partner should be open to the give and take. If you're looking for a new relationship, a new partner might be someone you already know. Sometimes love comes in ways that we don't expect. Keep an open mind.

Mind & Spirit: you're looking to achieve balance in all that you do on your path to your Higher Self. This is a period of contemplation before embarking upon a life changing path. You have a variety of options to actualize your vision so long as you give yourself space to act with courage. You have the power to write your next chapter so be bold and intentional with your goals.

Body: This is a great time to balance mind and body matters. So many of our needs are interconnected so it's important to pay extra close attention to your overall flow of energy to include chakras and balancing.

Money: 5 and 200 are key figures when making financial decisions. An idea for a creative opportunity has been set in motion and that you have the power to manifest your goals. This is also an indicator of a potentially life-changing trip or journey. This is a sign for you to prepare to step out of your comfort zone and embark upon a new path that will transform your life for the better. If you're looking for a new opportunity, you're about to discover a new career path or business venture that will be a bit unexpected but also complementary to your needs.

Travel: You're going to take a trip that will change the course of your life for the better.

Geography: Eastern Europe, Southwest Asia, Midwestern US, Central America, Polynesia

Locations: Sandy beaches, balconies, or a neighbor's home.

2 Of Wands Reversed

Overview: Two of Wands in reverse indicates that you might be feeling like you're out of your element. Perhaps you're trying to do too much at one time or staying in an environment that is not healthy for you. Examine what you need to succeed and to be happy and search out a different environment that best suits you. This is a time to find balance between practical concerns and creative endeavors. 12 is a key number. Instead of relying on one or two paths or goals you might need to consider diversifying your possibilities. Two of Wands in reverse indicates that you might be feeling a bit reluctant to make a decision or to organize areas of your life in ways that could help you accomplish your goals. What are you afraid of right now?

Love: A surprising new message concerning love is about to arrive. This is a time for gratitude and appreciating all that you have and all that you've accomplished, particularly concerning love in progress in self-compassion. It's also important to bear in mind that balance is an ongoing exercise that is never ending. You must maintain a balance and loving yourself as well as loving others in a healthy way. Even in the reverse position, this is still quite a positive omen. If you're currently in a relationship you can expect intimacy to improve as well as overall communication. If you're single, a new relationship is on the horizon. This is a wonderful time to trust in the power of the Universe to deliver real-time magic and a boost of vital energy.

Mind & Spirit: Remember that your authentic voice is the most important on your spiritual journey, so don't allow anyone to drown you out and attempt to impose their beliefs or opinions regarding your path. Trust in your own intuition.

Body: This is a time to focus on balance in mind and body, as well as being proactive regarding your physiological health. While it's great to educate yourself on health matters, it's also important not to ignore the advice of medical professionals. Don't be afraid of having conversations about your overall concerns with your doctor.

Money: This is still quite a positive omen regarding your professional endeavors and finances. However, if a current job position or project is coming to an end, be sure to be diplomatic about it. When it comes to money, this is not a time for risky gambling. An unexpected check or gift may be on its way to you, or you could see returns on a small investment.

Meditations: Are you not putting in enough effort to accomplish your goals? Do you need to summon up more courage? Are you doing too much at the same time?

3 Of Wands

Overview: Three of Wands indicates inspiration and guidance. you will soon experience inspiration and needed guidance. There will be an unexpected person who will appear in your life to offer unique insights and assistance to help advance your creative or professional endeavors. You might be feeling extra sensitive to the environment around you as well. Keep a keen eye out because opportunities that will benefit you will come from unlikely or unexpected sources. Three of Wands indicates a new road ahead and moving beyond your comfort zone. There is a possibility of traveling abroad, taking on a new opportunity, or starting a new education program. This card indicates that now is the time to move forward and accomplish your dreams.

Love: This is a positive omen regarding your romantic life, so long as your current relationships or potential ones involve balance. It's important that you maintain a mutual respect in your romantic relationships or keeping that in mind before starting new ones. If you feel that your voice is going unheard, it may be time to consider other options. If you're currently single, make sure that you feel loved and appreciated from the start and have the ability to balance your personal and professional life.

Mind & Spirit: It appears that your spiritual progress is going quite well. However, it's important to not become complacent on your journey. Always keep growing and learning. In general, this is a positive omen that you are taking steps in the right direction toward a promising new path. This is also a time for self-compassion and forgiveness. You've come a long way, and now it's time to shed the old skin and make way for transformation.

Body: Pay attention to issues regarding the lungs and skin. This card indicates overall positive news when it comes to your physiological health.

Money: It's important to feel appreciated and respected when it comes to your professional endeavors and business partnerships. There's nothing wrong with that. You've accomplished a lot and you deserve the rewards. This card also indicates positive new developments regarding your finances in long-term investments. This is an ideal time to save money but to also share where and when you can within reason. Think positively as your goals may manifest in ways that you never thought possible.

Travel: You may be taking the trip abroad where you will be negotiating with others for potential new business deal or partnership.

Geography: Eastern Europe, Southwest Asia, Midwestern US, Central America, New Caledonia

Locations: Seaside resorts or homes abroad, attics, pyramids, or terraces with panoramic views.

3 Of Wands Reversed

Overview: Three of Wands in reverse indicates that your present environment, whether it's professional or personal, maybe stifling you or even suffocating you. This may impact your overall health and wellness. Your senses might also not be so sharp at the moment. You must be careful of trusting the wrong sources of information regardless of intent. Be extra cautious of people or opportunities before proceeding. Three of Wands in reverse indicates potential delays in your current plans. There might be an unfortunate event that sets you back or that your heart really isn't in your current plans or projects. Ask yourself if this is what you really want.

Love: If you've been experiencing difficulties in your love life, things are about to take a positive turn. If you're currently in a relationship, you can expect an improvement in overall communication and connection. If you're currently looking for a romantic partnership this is a great time to meet new people who would complement your life in wonderful ways so long as you're not too judgmental. Keep an open mind.

Mind & Spirit: This is still a positive card when it comes to spiritual development and growth. You may find new discoveries in unexpected places which will change your life for the better.

Body: Three of Wands in reverse is still quite a positive card regarding your overall health so long as your vigilance in taking care of yourself.

Money: Now is the time to let your talents be known and to enjoy the spotlight. You might be embarking upon a new business venture that will allow you more independence and possibilities of taking your business abroad. Don't be afraid to connect with powerful people. Things should be looking up financially and will result from positive business partnerships rather than trying to go it alone.

Meditations: Are you feeling suffocated in your current circumstances? Are you ignoring resources or assistance around you? Are you expecting too much or too little?

4 Of Wands

Overview: Four of Wands is a card of peace and harmony, as well as new foundations for relationships, whether personal or professional. This card indicates that you can move in whatever direction is necessary to accomplish your goal especially when it comes to fostering peace and harmony in your own home. This also indicates the ability to move beyond into places that might not appear safe to others. There is a newfound peace growing around you. Pay attention to your third eye and trust your inner rhythms and cycles rather than the opinions of others. Four of Wands indicates a period of harmony enjoy. There could be a new birth or a wedding. This is also a good time to host a party or to invite friends over for a game night. Even if it doesn't feel like it right now, you will have reason to celebrate in the near future.

Love: This card indicates a positive new development in your romantic life. If you're currently in a relationship, you might find yourself feeling a sense of relief after investing time and energy in your partner. If you're single and looking for a new relationship, you might find success at meeting new people at a celebration, wedding, or some other happy occasion where many people are celebrating around you. Regardless of your relationship status, know that your mindset has a lot to do with manifesting what you want in your love life. Keep dreaming big and you will continue to grow in new and wonderful ways.

Mind & Spirit: This is a time to celebrate all your accomplishments and express gratitude to everyone that's helped you along the way. This is a great time to celebrate your successes and to also invite others you care about to share in your joy. You might have recently passed a life test with flying colors.

Body: This is a wonderful time to celebrate progress in your physical health. Maintain a positive mindset and you will go far.

Money: Pay attention to green or brown logos. This is a time to celebrate after a long period of hard work. This indicates an era of completion for you and making way for a new chapter where you will get to enjoy the fruits of your labor. You will find that abundance will allow you greater security in your personal life and allows you a lot more time in space to have fun. Express your gratitude to everyone who's helped you along the way, to include mentors and advisors who've helped you make wise decisions.

Travel: You will soon take a journey to take part in a celebration. This could be a wedding, a baby shower, a new birth, or another type of event that is surrounded by joy and love.

Geography: Eastern Europe, Southwest Asia, Midwestern US, Central America, Fiji

Locations: Cafés, buffets, hotel event spaces, castles, wedding venues, or chain restaurants.

4 Of Wands Reversed

Overview: The Four of Wands in reverse may indicate that someone is violating our boundaries and that you should be cautious no matter what their intent may be. Do not be careless around other people or in environments that could destroy your inner peace and happiness. At this time, you might feel that your talents are being wasted in a current circumstance and that where you're at right now is not a place that you want to build a foundation. This is not a time to be cocky or overconfident, and that you should look for other opportunities or alternatives so you can move on an adapt as you need to. Four of Wands in reverse indicates instability in one's home life or in a relationship. Do not run from change and remember to keep a positive mindset.

Love: You or a loved one might be feeling neglected in a current relationship. Whether you're in a relationship or single, there is an indication of obstacles standing in your way of making romantic progress. If you're in the process of planning a celebration, you might be anticipating delays or problems in moving forward due to romantic disagreements. You may also be dealing with someone who has problems in expressing gratitude for everyone who loves them in their life. Perhaps it's time for a change of perspective. Overall, Four of Wands in reverse indicates issues with maintaining harmony and balance in one's home life. This may also have to do an imbalance in one's personal and professional life that is reverberating in the romantic arena.

Mind & Spirit: This is not a time to be overly concerned with the judgment of others but to tune into your Higher Self and your authentic voice. You might be feeling as though your everyday routine has become a rut and you might be finding yourself feeling a bit unsatisfied with your progress. This is not a time to panic or to give way for anxiety, but to look for little ways to bring about balance in your home life.

Body: Issues with your throat, torso, or skin discoloration. News may still be quite positive regarding physiological health and it's important to maintain a positive outlook.

Money: You may still experience an unexpected windfall that will improve your financial status. Your work is appreciated but also consider how others have contributed to your progress and be grateful. Continue to save and put aside money to secure your financial future, but also make time to enjoy yourself and your progress.

Meditations: Is your current environment the best for you? Are you expressing gratitude for all that you have or accomplished? Are you being complacent in noticing red flags?

5 Of Wands

Overview: The Five of Wands indicates that you must do all that you can in times of struggle. This is not a time to be complacent or docile. If you're dealing with enemies or opposition, you need to respond assertively and aggressively as needed. If you establish your boundaries loud and clear, you're less likely to be violated again. Pay attention to your dreams at this time as they will offer additional insight on how to resolve conflict around you. Dreams will likely reveal hidden messages, problems, or even enemies that you may want to confront. If you're dealing with pests, whether physical or figurative, this is a time to be proactive. If you feel that you've been wronged, the most important next step is to decide how you respond. Overreacting is only likely to make problems worse. Figure out your best strategy for addressing problematic people or situations in ways they are going to be the most productive while being assertive in boundaries. Five of Wands indicates that friendly debates can result in plans manifesting. This is a good time to brainstorm, problem solve, and to keep your sense of humor.

Love: You might find yourself having to deal with conflicts or differences of opinion in matters of the heart. Whether you're in a relationship or single you might find that compromise comes in unexpected ways. This is not a time to be stubborn or to have a win-at-all-costs attitude. You are likely to experience small issues or petty squabbles rather than serious difficulties but it's important that you brainstorm when looking to resolve conflicts rather than acting up on impulse and saying something that you might regret. If you're single you might find that someone you consider to be a potential romantic partner might also have quite a few other options which could make way for competitive behavior. Show up as your best self as you are always enough and don't need to compare yourself with anyone. On the other hand, you might find yourself with plenty of romantic options.

Mind & Spirit: This is an important time to get grounded in your spiritual life and to go within and be still. This is not a time to compare your spiritual path with others but to simply be present.

Body: You might be experiencing some difficulty when it comes to getting answers regarding a long-standing health issue. This card also indicates the need to take a step back and reevaluate your goals and to consider whether the stress is worth it.

Money: You may be dealing with competition in the workplace or for improved financial opportunities. Remember to act with integrity and to look at your overall position as objectively as possible. Be patient on the path to achieving your goals.

Travel: You may be taking a journey where you are going to be participating in a competition, whether it's to compete for someone's affections or to compete in a tournament.

Geography: Eastern Europe, Southwest Asia, Midwestern US, Central America, Vanuatu, Papua New Guinea, Solomon Islands

Locations: Sports venues, martial arts studios, recreation centers, or public protests.

5 Of Wands Reversed

Overview: Five of Wands in reverse indicates that you might not be able to resolve the conflicts that you're currently facing. Sometimes it's best to take yourself out of a situation or distance yourself from others for everyone's benefit. Sometimes it's important to accept that things are not going to get any better or resolved anytime soon. Detaching yourself will at least provide a bit more perspective and peace in your life. Five of Wands in reverse indicates being avoidant of conflict or having difficult conversations. Don't be afraid to assert your point as your input can result in a positive outcome.

Love: Regarding your love life, Five of Wands in reverse indicates that any issues to be resolved will be to the benefit of your relationship or potential partnerships. If you're currently in a relationship, this is a great time to hash out any disagreements or disputes and to work together toward a compromise. In the process this will deepen intimacy. If you're single and looking for a potential romantic partner, you might be dealing with someone who is emotionally unavailable or is commitment phobic. This is someone who might present a great deal of difficulty to get to know, but it is entirely up to you to put in the time and effort.

Mind & Spirit: This is a time to put a lot of stock in your intuition as something doesn't seem quite right in your midst. No matter what difficulties you face right now, it's in your best interest to act with diplomacy. A mark of spiritual growth is how you handle yourself in the face of difficulties.

Body: You might be dealing with physiological pain at this time and would benefit from seeking out medical advice from a professional. You might have to make significant life changes in order to manage pain and be open to other treatment modalities.

Money: You might be experiencing comfort when it comes to your professional endeavors or business partnerships. If you find that unnecessary squabbles are standing in the way of your path to success, this might be a great time to reach out to someone who may be able to mediate and help all parties come to a resolution. This is not a time to engage in conflict, but to act with diplomacy. Don't make any risky decisions that can affect you in the long-term. If you're experiencing difficulty in your finances, this is a time to look at your situation objectively or to bring someone in to help you balance out your budget.

Meditations: Are you too entangled in drama to see the big picture? Is it time to take a step back in order to see things objectively? Are you being too defensive or reactive?

6 Of Wands

Overview: Six of Wands indicates hard work being rewarded. It is also a sign that good news is coming and that messages are likely to come through bringing us a renewed sense of optimism. Relationships, whether personal or professional, are likely to improve at this time and efforts after a long period of hard work are about to be rewarded. Pay attention to the numbers 6 and 12. Within two to three months, you're likely to see new opportunities and circumstances emerge as well as rewards for all your effort. Six of Wands indicates that you may be experiencing admiration for recent accomplishments and hard work. You're likely to find success in accomplishing your goals, and others around you will take notice with admiration.

Love: This is a positive card indicating overcoming obstacles and a current or potential partnership. Things are moving along in positive new directions and will be a cause for celebration. If you're currently in a relationship this may indicate an improvement in overall intimacy. If you're single and looking for a romantic partner, know that someone who fits the criteria you've been holding onto is about to show up in your life. Maintain a positive mindset and be open to wonderful new possibilities.

Mind & Spirit: This card indicates that you're on a positive path regarding your spiritual development and growth. Keep working on being your best self and tuning into Source. You have many wonderful talents and skills to share with the world, so continue to work on yourself and be open to new possibilities.

Body: This card indicates positive new developments regarding your health or the health of someone you love. Maintain a positive mindset.

Money: When it comes to finances, you're likely to see an improvement. However, it's going to be important to not overspend with any new increases or windfalls. It's important to save and to put money aside in case of emergencies. In terms of professional endeavors, you might find that your goals are realized in ways that are bigger and better than you had imagined. Know that you are appreciated and just continue to do amazing things.

Travel: You are likely to take a journey where you are going to celebrate the fruits of your labor.

Geography: Eastern Europe, Southwest Asia, Midwestern US, Central America, Australia

Locations: Marketplaces, awards ceremonies, busy downtown areas, or parades.

6 Of Wands Reversed

Overview: Six of Wands in reverse indicates that you might be giving up too soon. If you continue to try and push things too hard right now it might lead to great disappointment. The timing is just not right. Six of Wands in reverse indicates that your current plans might not manifest in a way that you expect, and this could impact your own reputation. It is up to you to determine this outcome. Also ask yourself if you are standing in your own way.

Love: This is not a time to be overly aggressive when it comes to matters of the heart. Something might feel a bit off about timing with the current relationship or a potential new partnership. Just know that romance can happen in unexpected ways, so don't be too tied to one specific outcome. While this card in reverse is still a positive omen, it just means that you might be experiencing setbacks in interpersonal relationships, or you may be dealing with someone who is quite jealous. It's important to tune into your intuition and to trust what messages the Universe is sending you. If you're in a committed relationship, there might be a sense of fear coming from you or your partner. When we judge we have no room to love, and someone might be projecting their insecurities onto you or vice versa. If you're looking for a relationship, a negative mindset might have been dominating your psyche. It's important to alter your perspective and remember that you are worthy of love and deserve a partnership that complements your life.

Mind & Spirit: If you've been waiting for a sign, now is the time to pay close attention to the messages the Universe is sending your way. You might also consider getting feedback from others regarding their own spiritual journey. You don't have to accept anyone's life lessons for yourself, but you might learn important insights by learning what someone has done on the path to enlightenment.

Body: This is an important time to consider what you're doing to benefit your overall health. Sometimes it involves changing a simple daily living habit or trying something completely new to give yourself a boost of energy. If you're not getting your health questions answered, persevere, and keep trying.

Money: You may feel as though you are experiencing unnecessary difficulties with problematic people who are projecting their personal issues onto you in your professional life. This is a time to take a step back and try to handle things diplomatically or to have someone else mediate. If you're looking out for new opportunities try to learn as much as you can before accepting any offers. Things are not always what they seem. When it comes to money this is not a time to get complacent about your spending or when it comes to paying off any debt. You may also find ways to earn additional income that could significantly boost her financial status.

Meditations: Are you trying to show off too soon? Are you putting in enough effort? Are you losing faith in yourself?

7 Of Wands

Overview: Seven of Wands is a card that indicates personal empowerment and resources. This is a time to draw upon your inner strength and resources. This is also a time to learn how to protect yourself and your movements, whether literal or figurative. You will also have the benefit of numerous advantages in resolving conflicts or overcoming difficulty with success and recognition for your efforts on the horizon. Know how to divide your time to conserve your inner strength. Seven of Wands indicates that success is at hand and that you have every right to feel self-confident. This is also about giving yourself credit for achievement and that others around you might be envious.

Love: Now might be a time to take a stand in your love life, whether you're currently in a relationship or single. This is not a time to give in to expectations regarding dogma or tradition, but what really matters to you and can make you happy in the long-term. This is a time where it's important to believe in yourself and to be courageous enough to set healthy boundaries and enforce them when necessary. Don't back down when it comes to loving yourself better. Try new approaches or new methods to improve your romantic life.

Mind & Spirit: It's important to take a stand when it comes to preserving your peace. This is a time to be courageous and know that you have everything that you need at your disposal to accomplish anything on your path to success. This is time to let go of fear-based thinking and make way for a new energy that nurtures courage and action.

Body: You may be dealing with concerns regarding your physiological health but know that your worries maybe unfounded or not as bad as you thought. Be sure to check in with a medical professional if you have any concerns.

Money: A key number is 50 when it comes to financial increases or professional decisions. Positive changes are coming to your professional life so long as you're willing to put in the work. This might be a time to consider all your options in leveling up in your career. This is also a great time for financial increases that might come from unexpected sources, or you may be anticipating a check that turns out to be bigger than you imagined. This is not a time to spend, but to conserve your resources and think wisely about the future.

Travel: You may be taking a trip that is fun but one that also tests your courage.

Geography: Eastern Europe, Southwest Asia, Midwestern US, Central America, Australia

Locations: Mountains, indoor rock-climbing, or endurance tests.

7 Of Wands Reversed

Overview: When Seven of Wands is in reverse, it is a sign that you might have gotten too far away from your roots as well as your own personal power and forgetting what brought you to this point in life. You might also not be completely noticing opportunities when they manifest. You might be hesitating to move forward and act upon said opportunities by allowing fear to take the wheel. Seven of Wands in reverse indicates that you might be feeling vulnerable and having issues with your self-esteem. Maybe it's time to take a step back, especially if drama is involved, and reevaluate ways to build upon your self-esteem.

Love: You may feel a sense of powerlessness in your romantic life or that you may be choosing the wrong battles. If you're currently in a relationship, you might find yourself backing down from standing up for yourself – which is not recommended. Loving yourself also includes enforcing your boundaries. However, if you find yourself engaging in arguments that do not align with your values, it may be time to take a step back and reevaluate your priorities and see if a current situation is no longer serving your best interests. If you're currently in a relationship, you might be feeling a bit ambivalent about what to do next to resolve a current relationship dilemma. You might have difficulty in expressing yourself or are wondering if it's the time or place to bring up a difficult topic. If you're looking for a new relationship, the best advice is to get out and look for new ways to meet new people. Remember that people are more than just a series of checklists and to keep an open mind when it comes to a potential new partnership. Remember that love is not just looking at each other but looking in the same direction.

Mind & Spirit: This is an important time to be still and to go within rather than to talk ad nauseum about your journey or to spend too much time in conversation about it. Many answers to your questions can be found in meditation and being present.

Body: You may be experiencing health issues associated with oral hygiene or your tongue. You might also be experiencing a degree of stress or anxiety that could be contributing to physiological symptoms. Seek out the guidance of a medical professional.

Money: This is not a time to be indecisive, and you should act upon the best options regarding professional decisions in business ventures. Trust your intuition in making the right decision. You may feel a bit unclear about the path ahead when it comes to your finances or professional opportunities, but you may benefit from seeking out the advice and guidance of an expert. You might also experience delays in receiving payments, bonuses, or a return on an investment. If you feel that you're not appreciated in your professional life, now may be the time to look for new opportunities.

Meditations: Are you establishing and maintaining healthy boundaries? Are you allowing fear to prevent you from making substantial progress?

8 Of Wands

Overview: The Eight of Wands indicates rapid movement. There will be warp speed regarding your endeavors and goals and you can continue to see rapid movement for quite some time. Hang on tight once you see the Eight of Wands as things are going to move beyond your control. Your goals are within reach, and you will be able to get closer to them to capture opportunities soon. This is now a time for elevated senses, or you can detect the subtlest of vibrations around you. It is best to not take anything at face value but rely on your other senses to tell you when to act and how to do so. Trusting your inner voice and your intuition will help you become more successful. Eight of Wands indicates changes that are coming whether or not you're ready and not to hesitate. Make sure that you complete every task on your to-do list as change is unfolding at a rapid pace. You will need to keep up.

Love: You can expect swift action, progress, and movement when it comes to the Eight of Wands in your love life. Once things are set in motion there is no stopping it. So be sure that what you have in mind to build your ideal relationship is clear and detailed before declaring your intentions to the Universe. This is also an indication that any disputes or difficulties in current relationships or potential romantic partnerships will soon be resolved or confronted. Regardless of your relationship status, be careful about rushing to make any permanent decisions. In any case, this card is about quickly changing life events that will feel like a whirlwind. On the other hand, be on guard about being forceful in relationships and to give people their space. You might be ready to move forward but someone else might not be, or vice versa.

Mind & Spirit: If you're anticipating answers from the Universe you can expect to get those messages quite soon. This is a time to trust in the Universe and hold on for the ride as quick changes are coming.

Body: You are likely to get the results of health tests quite soon. It's important to maintain a positive mindset and to do your best to be vigilant in taking care of your health.

Money: This is not a time to be too forceful in enacting change. You can expect swift changes to take place in your professional life and your finances, some of which might be out of your control. You may also be taking a trip by airplane to begin new business ventures. You might also be anticipating news or results regarding new opportunities. Know that change is coming quick and events that have been set in motion are now starting to come into fruition. If you're dealing with any workplace difficulties, you can expect that they will be resolved soon.

Travel: You may receive unexpected news which requires air travel and new opportunities.

Geography: Eastern Europe, Southwest Asia, Midwestern US, Central America, Australia

Locations: Sporting events, marathon sites, mountains, airports, or hotels.

8 Of Wands Reversed

Overview: Eight of Wands in reverse indicates that there may be some delays in your plans. Unseen forces could disrupt progress. You might be also trying to do too much at one time so it's important to adjust your plans and goals accordingly. In terms of long-term plans, you might see changes within three to four years and for short-term plans by the following summer. This card in reverse indicates that any plans that you might have could experience a potential delay. If you find that your energy feels a bit all over the place, take some time to meditate and reflect on your own needs and goals.

Love: You might be experiencing setbacks in your romantic life or not seeing things manifest in ways that you thought. Some of these delays, whether in a current relationship or a potential new partnership, might be causing you a bit of frustration and disappointment. Perhaps you've been pushing too hard, too fast, and too soon. This is a time to take a step back and reevaluate your priorities. This is also a warning to watch how you communicate with others. Take a deep breath and think about what you want to say before you say it, or you might be dealing with unnecessary misunderstandings. If you're waiting on messages or responses from others, don't sit around waiting for someone else to act. Use this time to work on yourself.

Mind & Spirit: You may be experiencing a burst of energy which may be causing you difficulty when it comes to focusing or meditating. Try not to be too impulsive in decision-making. This is a time to go within and look for answers. If you're looking for swift messages, the Universe can provide only if you commit to stillness.

Body: Be careful with short-distance travel and take your time, even if you're running late to avoid potential delays or accidents. It's better to arrive safely than not at all.

Money: This is not a time to push too hard or try to force any decisions to be made. Pushing too hard in any certain direction is likely to backfire. If you're waiting on a response for a potential new opportunity, this is a time to take a step back and use the time to do something productive. When it comes to your finances, know that long-term success requires long-term hard work. Luck only seems like luck from the outside, but it's merely a combination of when preparation meets opportunity. Do your best to prepare for such success and to have everything lined up, so when the opportunity appears you can act quickly.

Meditations: Are you hesitating to take on opportunities due to fear? Do you need to slow down and break free of bad habits and old thought patterns before proceeding? Are you counting your eggs before they hatch?

9 Of Wands

Overview: Nine of Wands indicates maintaining control, resources, and discretion. This is also a time to mind your own business and protect your own affairs. Be careful not to overextend yourself physically, professionally, or personally. If you feel that you're being attacked, maintain your position, and defend it. This is not a time to demonstrate or reveal any personal weaknesses. This is a time to strike back as needed, protect what is yours whether it is possessions or secrets. In persevering you will successfully protect what's yours. Nine of wands indicates having difficulties in completing a task or difficulties in moving forward. This is also a sign for you to persevere as you are close to the end of a struggle. Keep an open mind.

Love: This is not a time to rush anything when it comes to love or to be hypercritical of your partner or potential partner. It's important at this time that everyone has space to breathe and reflect. If you're not in a relationship, consider the timing and if you've given yourself enough time to heal old wounds. This might be the ideal time to get centered and to give yourself the love you need before starting anything new. When you love yourself, it will radiate from you and attract the right person. There are no shortcuts on this path, you must do the work to include shadow work in order to truly accept and love yourself. When it comes to dealing with any type of conflict it's important to pause, breathe, and think before you speak.

Mind & Spirit: You might be tempted to take the path of least resistance or shortcuts on the way to your Higher Self, and this is not advised. This is a time for introspection and self-compassion. You have all the tools and resources at your disposal to accomplish your spiritual goals. Take some time to write down new affirmations in place your intentions with the Universe.

Body: You may have issues in balancing out certain aspects of your physical health. Additional stress reducing activities may be of benefit but be sure to check in with a trusted medical or mental health professional.

Money: You might be experiencing interpersonal difficulties in your professional life. It's important to maintain a diplomatic approach in dealing with problematic people. If you're looking for new opportunities, this is a positive omen for new changes ahead. This might also be an indication that you should be looking out for new opportunities as a current chapter might be coming to a close. This is an important time to be strategic in your budget and savings.

Travel: Be careful in planning travel that revolves around a self-fulfilling prophecy. Make sure that the trip that you're embarking on is well thought-out and well-planned.

Geography: Arizona, Eastern Europe, Southwest Asia, Midwestern US, Central America, Australia

Locations: Deserts, mountains, retreats, guarded entries, or security offices.

9 Of Wands Reversed

Overview: Nine of Wands in reverse indicates that you feel out of sync with your natural rhythms. You might be trying to force something that is not healthy and may be feeling burned out. This is a time to take a step back and reassess the situation as well as focusing on self-preservation. Nine of Wands in reverse indicates that you should not blame others for holding you back. If there are obstacles standing in your way, ask yourself what lesson this is trying to teach you. Are you possibly holding yourself back out of fear?

Love: You may feel that something is off regarding your romantic life. You might be at a point where you're wondering if you're fighting for the right things in a relationship. You might also be experiencing difficulties in resolving conflicts within a current relationship. It might not be helpful for you at this time to be holding on to fixed ideas and it's even less ideal to try to force anyone to see things your way. This is a time to act with love and compassion. If you're currently looking for a relationship, exercising patience and kindness is to your benefit at this time. This is not a time to rush into anything new, but to take things day by day.

Mind & Spirit: This is not a time to look back upon your past with regret or to dredge up old wounds. This is a time to act with self-compassion. You may be feeling out of sync with your current cycles and wondering if this feeling of burnout will ever go away. This is a good time to ask for the advice of someone with experience in what you're dealing with. Bear in mind that what you've tried before might not work again this time. No matter what you do, just ensure that you're setting healthy boundaries.

Body: This is a time to focus on stress management in order to prevent it from having an impact on your physical health. Talk with your doctor about different ways you can alleviate tension to improve your overall wellness.

Money: You might currently be concerned with your financial situation and how to balance your budget. Worrying will do you no good. This is not a time to partake in any get-rich-quick schemes or fast solutions to long-term problems. You might also be feeling stress over your current professional life and may be having difficulties in managing your emotions. Seek guidance when and where necessary.

Meditations: Are you properly maintaining control of your situation? Are you exposing yourself to people that mean to do you harm? Are you affectively standing open the face of adversity or bending?

10 Of Wands

Overview: Ten of Wands indicates moving through pressure. Right now, it's important to carry on whether it comes to responsibilities in your life or with plans. It's important to keep going no matter how slow it may seem. Sometimes things need to work out in their own time and it's important to trust that things do happen when you're ready. There are all sorts of reasons why things are happening. You will move through any difficult circumstance and will overcome any obstacle. Ten of Wands indicates a bit of caution. Perhaps you've bitten off more than you can chew and may need time to reflect on what you need and if you need assistance.

Love: You may feel as though you're a carrying excessive burdens in your love life, whether you're single or attached. You may feel that taking on many responsibilities has impacted your romantic life. Or you may find that your partner and their responsibilities are affecting your connection. In any case, you might be experiencing a rough patch that could be remedied through communicating needs that might have been overlooked. This is not a time to become complacent as problems arise. If you're single in looking, you may be feeling like you're doing way too much or that you're way too busy to give love any serious thought. This may be a time to draw healthy boundaries that can create space for your love life.

Mind & Spirit: This is not a time to ignore assistance when it's offered, as you may have been dealing with carrying a significant load, emotionally or professionally, and could use the help. This is a time to focus on self-care but also accepting help.

Body: Stress and overwork may be impacting your health in a negative way. This is a time for conscientious self-care and to seek out help as needed. After a long period of hard work, it might be nice to treat yourself for a day at the spa or a quick getaway to unwind.

Money: You may be experiencing a period of overwork which may lead to burnout if you're not careful. When it comes to your finances this is the time to save and avoid overspending or frivolous investments. This is a time to be strategic and careful where you put your time, energy, and money in a way that allows you to breathe in the long-term.

Travel: You may be taking a trip in order to alleviate stress which is much needed.

Geography: Eastern Europe, Southwest Asia, Midwestern US, Central America, Australia

Locations: Sweatshops, workplaces, or offices with long wait periods.

10 Of Wands Reversed

Overview: When Ten of Wands in reverse, it's a sign that you need to slow down as life may be getting too hectic. You will have plenty of time to accomplish your goals, but you need to also be patient. Progress toward success is one step at a time. It's time to return to your roots, the basics, and remember where you've come from and how far you've made it. Use your talents and skills in the proper way. Ten of Wands and reverse is an indicator of possible procrastination that may lead to larger problems if unattended.

Love: If you're currently in a relationship, it's time to get serious about being completely honest in any ongoing pressures or difficulties you may be experiencing. It's important to be transparent in your intentions with one another, even if it includes an affair. Ten of Wands in reverse indicates possible deception and infidelity or recent changes in behavior that may lead to suspicion. If you're single and looking for a relationship, this may be a time to focus on yourself rather than putting yourself out there for something new. A time will come when an opportunity presents itself – it's just not now.

Mind & Spirit: This is an important time to guard your energy from any external negative influences. Perhaps stress has been attacking you in a variety of ways, and you might have been letting your spiritual firewall down. It's time to get vigilant about taking care of yourself.

Body: This is a time where stress may be pushing you towards breaking point. Exercise caution and consult with a trusted professional to discuss your current concerns. This is not a time to neglect your needs or your health.

Money: If you're currently dissatisfied with your financial situation or your professional life, this might be the time to think strategically about the future and look for new opportunities. Do your best to stay away from any interpersonal professional drama and focus on yourself. This is a time to conserve all your resources and to not make any significant risks with your money because it may be important to prepare for the near future and potential hardship.

Meditations: Are you taking on other people's burdens and not your own? Are you ignoring your own needs? Are you being too impatient?

Page Of Wands

Overview: The Page of Wands indicates news of change. This card indicates a possible change of environment and that such changes will be positive. You begin to see that things are coming out clearly and that you can trust your inner voice. This card indicates that coming opportunities are there for the taking. Within a day you're likely to hear of the beginning of new changes. Opportunities that present themselves should be acted upon within a day or they may pass you by. Although movement throughout life might have felt slow, know that when it comes to opportunities you must act quickly. Page of Wands overall signifies that good news is coming and this could represent a vibrant person who loves pushing a project or plans forward. They are free-spirited and have the energy to take on the world.

Love: You may be receiving messages regarding your love life, especially as it pertains to someone with a lot of energy and creativity. If you're currently in a relationship, this is a time to figure out whether this romance is worth saving or if you should stick it out for the long-term. It might be important to put a time stamp on it. If you're not finding mutual give and take in a partnership, it might be time to cut your losses and move on. If you're unattached and looking for love, someone with a lot of energy and a flair for adventure might be entering your life soon. This is a person who is enthusiastic and motivated to complete their goals.

Mind & Spirit: This is an excellent time to tap into your creative energies and figure out how that might play into your overall spiritual development and wellness. Tap into your Higher Self and Source to channel inspiration into wonderful new projects.

Body: You might need to reinvigorate your health and wellness routine in order to improve your overall physiological health. This is a time to be assertive and proactive.

Money: You may find a sudden new burst of energy when it comes to your professional endeavors and your finances. If you're expecting a message regarding either one, you're likely to hear the news within the next few weeks. This is an ideal time to think strategically about the future and to think about on all the goals and dreams that you had in the past period what dreams still apply? And what are you willing to risk to turn those dreams into reality?

Travel: This is a time for new adventure and a journey that will take you abroad and put you in touch with exciting new people.

Geography: Egypt, Eastern Europe, Southwest Asia, Midwestern US, Central America, Australia, southwest United States

Locations: Fitness studios, desert retreats, group fitness meetups, or schools.

Page Of Wands Reversed

Overview: When Page of Wands in reverse it indicates that you might be trying to move too quickly or getting ahead of yourself. You might need to slow down and reassess where you're coming from. You might also notice that your mood or the moods of others are quite erratic at this time. page of wands in reverse indicates that a current endeavor is stagnant. There might be unexpected complications or unfavorable news. You might also be dealing with someone who is being overly aggressive and immature.

Love: Mood instability is likely to impact the current or upcoming relationship. You might be receiving an unsavory message regarding your love life. This is not a time to be indecisive about the next steps ahead. If you're intent on saving a relationship. This is a time to get to know each other better and talk seriously about your expectations in a relationship. If you're single, a friend or a loved one may have bad news about a potential new love interest. While you should always give people a chance to speak for themselves, you should also not ignore red flags.

Mind & Spirit: This is a time to trust in your Higher Self and to speak loudly with your authentic voice. This is a great time, even with this card in the reverse, for creative projects to be manifested in wonderful ways. This is a time to go within and to channel the creative muse.

Body: It appears that you have the resources and experts around you that you require to get answers regarding your physiological health. This is not a time to go it alone but to be open to different options in different ways that you can connect with others while improving your health.

Money: The Page of Wands in reverse is still quite a positive card when it comes to financial prospects, especially from unexpected sources. Whatever windfall you might experience, be sure to conserve some of your resources but to also help others in need with discernment. This is not a time to be indecisive or to anticipate messages coming through as quick as you had hoped for. Be patient and things will manifest in its own time.

Meditations: Are you becoming oversensitive? Are you reading into things out of fear or insecurity and not perceiving things as they are? Are you overreacting? Are you ignoring red flags?

Knight Of Wands

Overview: The knight of wands indicates using your instincts an impulse is strategically. this is a time for rapid decision-making, change, and assertive action. Something within you is being awakened, in creative energies are all around and quite strong. This is not a time to be complacent, this is the time to act. You're going to see a window of opportunity occurring within eight months and you must act quickly. This will have long-lasting, powerful effects on your life. You can use your skills and abilities to initiate changes as needed and also figure out what needs to come to an end. Knight of Wands indicates a raw power in great confidence. This is a very enthusiastic person with a lot of energy and clear thinking. Key numbers are 7, 8, 100, 150, 200, 350, 5000.

Love: If you're currently in a relationship, it might be ideal to be as intentional and clear as possible when it comes to communicating your needs and boundaries. This is not a time to engage in misunderstandings but to be brief and concise in communicating what you need and want. If you're single and looking to meet a potential new partner, you may benefit from meeting them through a professional event or through mutual contacts. The Knight of Wands is high energy and is not afraid to take risks. You might be on the lookout for someone who is full of charisma and confidence. While they may have difficulties in focusing their attention you may have what they need to maintain balance. However, be cautious of anyone that is too reckless in their behavior and too impulsive.

Mind & Spirit: You may benefit from new approaches to kickstarting your spiritual journey. Keep an open mind and try to look at things from a new perspective.

Body: Knight of Wands generally indicates good news when it comes to health in the short-term. However, you must be careful and over exerting yourself to avoid exercise-related injuries. Be gentle with yourself.

Money: You may be receiving positive news regarding a new business partnership or professional opportunity, especially as it pertains to travel. Your finances may also be on the upswing at this time. However, it's important that you don't throw to caution to the wind and start spending recklessly.

Travel: You may need to travel long-distance for a professional opportunity or a new business partnership.

Geography: Egypt, Eastern Europe, Southwest Asia, Midwestern US, Central America, New Zealand

Locations: Racquetball courts, horse races, airport lounges, or animal shelters.

Knight Of Wands Reversed

Overview: Knight of Wands in reverse indicates that everything you're doing can take on great power. However, you must be careful of how you use that power with others. Be careful of using words that are harsh as diplomacy is your friend right now. Everything said or done has a greater impact and effect right now. Be cautious of what you say and do and how it affects others. Your words or the words of others have the power to destroy. Knight of Wands in reverse is a warning to look out for impatient people or overlooking important information.

Love: If you're currently in a relationship, you might be experiencing difficulty in resolving ongoing conflicts that are possibly quite trivial. Try to take a step back and get some perspective and see whether or not either of you are projecting other external factors into the relationship. Is it really about toothpaste? Or is it about something serious that you're neglecting to discuss? If you're currently looking for a relationship, proceed with caution with a person who seems like a perfect 10 or close to it. This person may have commitment issues or may be frightened away by trying to force a relationship.

Mind & Spirit: You may be receiving a message that answers a burning question that you may have had about your spiritual path and your life purpose. Your patience in waiting will soon pay off. You might find that a guide or someone with a lot more experience may assist you in this time in helping you see the bigger picture and tapping into your intuition. Be intentional about your goals and affirmations, and watch the Universe deliver in real-time.

Body: This is not a time to overexert yourself physically but to take things one day at a time. Overdoing anything at this point will likely lead to avoidable sports-related injuries. Focus on being your healthiest self rather than aspiring to an unrealistic ideal.

Money: You may be dealing with a bit of conflict when it comes to your finances in your professional life. This is a time to maintain a positive mindset and to handle disagreements with diplomacy instead of impulsive responses. This is also a time to rethink your financial situation and to make logical moves toward long term stability. If you are experiencing any setbacks, now may be the time to step away and gain some perspective.

Meditations: Are you letting drama get in the way of living your life? Are there envious eyes around you? Are you responding to opportunities when you need to?

Queen Of Wands

Overview: Queen of wands indicates the power of creativity and inner strength. This is a time where balance will arrive unexpectedly. However, this will come as a result of your hard work, talent, and creativity. What you do now will set the stage of a foundation that will impact your life for the next five to ten years. Within the next ninety days to four months, you'll discover new opportunities coming your way that should take just as long. Your instincts will be very sharp, and you should trust your inner voice. You will have the opportunity to tap into your intuition and your Higher Self. New birth is near, whether literal or figurative, as is success. Queen of Wands is a person with a courageous and bold personality. This is someone who is vibrant and high energy with impeccable taste for the pleasures in life. They're very creative and highly intelligent. This is also someone who can stand up to any challenge and enjoys learning new things.

Love: Queen of Wands is generally a positive sign in your romantic life. You may be dealing with someone who is very creative, passionate, an confident. This is someone who has a mature energy and is the life of the party – not to mention sex appeal. charismatic in nature and have the power to influence and manipulate people and other variables to their benefit. If you're currently looking for a relationship this is also a positive sign. You are likely to meet someone who challenges you in a positive way. However, you must also put forth the effort in order to meet new people. this is also quite a fertile time, literally and figuratively, so plan accordingly.

Mind & Spirit: You may be energized now more than ever to embark upon a new spiritual path that will be transformative in a wonderfully positive way. Before making any impulsive decisions it's important to pause and take stock of what's important and if any major changes align with your Higher Self.

Body: You should feel a burst of energy and feel proactive about your overall health. This is also a fertile period for making things happen, literally or figuratively.

Money: You may benefit from the sage advice of a professional expert who could help shape your career and financial stability. They are high energy but also might come across self-centered. It is not advised to get carried away with spending at this time, no matter how tempting it may be. In your professional life you may be getting a lot of things done quicker than you ever have before, and you may be tempted to spoil yourself as a reward. Just be mindful of your spending, but you can also have a good time.

Travel: You may be taking a trip where you get recentered an reenergized that opens up a new creative streak in your life. Enjoy it.

Geography: Eastern Europe, Southwest Asia, Midwestern US, Central America, New Zealand

Locations: Fields of sunflowers, deserts, places to watch the leaves change in fall, nightclubs, or aesthetician locations.

Queen Of Wands Reversed

Overview: Queen of Wands in reverse indicates that you might not be paying attention to new creative opportunities at your doorstep. It seems that you're not taking advantage of impulses and new endeavors. You also need to exercise caution that you might not be seeing everything as it is. There may be hidden dangers in your environment especially ones that you seem to trust. There may be a reason you're not feeling 100% about what's going on around you. If you're not careful you may be dragged into a terrible situation where it'll be difficult to recover. Queen of Wands in reverse indicates that you should ask yourself if anything is holding you back from accomplishing your goal. This is also an indication that you have what it takes to succeed.

Love: If you're currently in a relationship, you might be dealing with someone who is trying to meddle in your love life. This could be a relative or someone trying to involve themselves in your relationship in a malicious way. If this is a family member of your partner, be sure to be as diplomatic as possible and to be compassionate despite their approach. Even if someone comes across as self-centered and perhaps mean, consider that their behavior has less to do with you and more with their personal problems. If you're single and looking for a relationship, you may meet someone new through a mentor or trusted advisor.

Mind & Spirit: Queen of Wands in reverse indicates not feeling completely self-aware of your own power. Be careful that you're not overreacting in situations that may lead you to come across as cold hearted and crass. This is a time to be extra vigilant in how you're approaching situations and communicating with others. Remember to come from a place of compassion for yourself and others.

Body: You may be dealing with unresolved anger that may be affecting your overall health. No matter what you're feeling, it's important to own your feelings and to express it in a healthy way. If you're holding onto any resentments, now may be a time to seek out professional guidance on how best you may heal those old wounds. If you're dealing with any fertility issues, now may be the time to seek out a specialist to address any of your concerns.

Money: Now is not the time to engage in any frivolous spending, especially if you're trying to fill a void within. This is a time to conserve your resources and save for a rainy day. When it comes to professional endeavors, you might be dealing with someone who is being unreasonably difficult and presenting obstacles where none should exist. Do your best to remain objective in dealing with this person as their issues are not necessarily personal with you but reflect their own inner turmoil.

Meditations: Are you ignoring your intuition? Are you letting your emotions get the best of you? Are you lending your trust to people who don't deserve it?

King Of Wands

Overview: The King of Wands indicates rapid decision making and action. Opportunities for advancement are very close and you should be prepared. Whatever might seem foolish to other people will prove to be successful to you at this time. This is a time to remain alert to any subtle signs or movements around you and to trust in the vibrations. Do not be distracted by anything people say, this is a time to trust your own perceptions regardless of how they appear. The King of Wands indicates a person who is very entrepreneurial and has the capability of transforming ideas into its highest potential. This is a person who is in search of perfection and has laser-like focus on the road to achieving their goal. This is a person who either represents you or someone that you know who has great focus when it comes to getting things done.

Love: King of Wands is generally a positive card when it comes to love and romance. This is someone who is also passionate and charismatic, with seemingly boundless energy. This could represent someone you're involved with or someone that you could be dealing with in a potential romantic partnership. It could also indicate an aspect of yourself to nurture. If you're currently in a relationship, this may indicate positive new developments that are filled with a sudden burst of energy and a need for adventure. Maybe it's time to try something new to spice things up! If you're currently looking for a relationship, you might encounter someone who speaks enthusiastically with their authentic voice. They can be both passionate but also have somewhat of a temper, so be sure to define your boundaries early as well as any potential deal-breakers.

Mind & Spirit: You may be feeling adventurous as of late and excited to accomplish your goals. It's important to maintain a positive mindset and to put your dreams into action. Wonderful things can manifest as a result. It appears that you are on a positive path to accomplishing your spiritual goals, but don't try to put the cart before the horse. Remember that significant spiritual progress results from putting in hard work.

Body: This is generally a good card regarding physiological health as well as recovering from any injuries. Be sure to keep your emotions in check, particularly when it comes to anger and resentment. It's important to express not repress.

Money: When it comes to finances, you might want to exercise caution in making any long-term decisions that could affect your stability. You might also uncover a new skill or creative project that could lead to a new income stream. Be open minded when considering all possibilities to improve your overall state in life. You might also encounter someone who could be a wonderful mentor.

Travel: You might take an exciting new trip that feels like an adventure in order to learn a new skill.

Geography: India, Sri Lanka, Eastern Europe, Southwest Asia, Midwestern US, Central America, New Zealand

Locations: Creative or entrepreneurial workshops, or popular nature sites near a large city.

King Of Wands Reversed

Overview: The King of Wands in reverse indicates that you may be blind to what's going on around you, including opportunities for advancement. You may be allowing fear to prevent you from acting upon the appropriate course of action. If you're not sure how to act, don't act at all. Make sure that you have all the facts first before deciding what to do next. However, if you do see an opportunity that is right for you, failing to act could prove disastrous. 15 is a key number. King of Wands in reverse may serve as a warning that someone is trying to manipulate you or that you might be making a quick decision with negative consequences.

Love: Be on your guard with anyone who is trying to force themselves into your life or attempting to coerce you into accepting a way of life that you don't agree with. This is still a good omen when it comes to love, so long as you exercise and enforce your boundaries. While someone may be very charismatic, you have to ensure that your needs are being met, too. Whether you're in a relationship or looking for one, it's important to also put yourself first and not sideline your own goals and dreams in order to make someone happy. Love is not losing yourself, but a call to maturity. If this person doesn't align with your goals to grow into your Higher Self, you might want to consider other options.

Mind & Spirit: You may encounter an older advisor who may help you out on your spiritual journey. While you are in constant search of answers, know that many of the solutions that you're looking for and asking of the Universe already exists within. Take some time for meditation and needed introspection to figure out what it is that you really want.

Body: You may experience difficulty with breathing or cardiac issues. Animal bites are also possible at this time. It might be beneficial to seek out someone who could assist you in your overall fitness and nutrition goals.

Money: You may benefit from seeking the counsel of an expert when it comes to financial planning. There is nothing wrong with asking for help. Even if you have extra money on the side, it might be ideal to invest it for a nest egg in the long-term. When it comes to professional endeavors you might be dealing with difficult people who maybe borderline inappropriate. While it's important to keep up your guard, if someone is crossing a line with you, it's important to remedy the situation as quickly as possible.

Meditations: Are you acting too impulsively? Do you really have all the facts? Is someone around you abusing your trust? Is there a hidden danger in your immediate environment?

CONCLUSION

It is our sincere hope that you have thoroughly enjoyed this tarot journey with Modern Tarot. On your own journey through connecting with your selected decks, know that you are part of a community that is in constant search of new knowledge and enlightenment. We encourage you to continue your journey in learning new techniques, spreads, and ways to find balance in your life. May you continue to learn and grow from reading all the guides and signposts along the way and embrace all that is beautiful in your Higher Self.

RESOURCES

There are a variety of wonderful resources and guides out there waiting to be discovered. Your journey through tarot will be rewarded through uncovering these wonderful treasures that provide helpful tips and insights while traveling on your path to your Higher Self. The following is a list of resources that helped shape this book and you may find them to be quite helpful as well:

BOOKS & JOURNALS

- Auger, E. E. (2019). Pamela Colman Smith: The Untold Story by Stuart R. Kaplan with Mary K. Greer, Elizabeth Foley O'Connor, and Melinda Boyd Parsons. Mythlore: A Journal of JRR Tolkien, CS Lewis, Charles Williams, and Mythopoeic Literature, 37(2), 21.

- Crowley, A. (1944). Book of Thoth:(Egyptian Tarot) (Vol. 3, No. 5). Weiser Books.

- Decker, R., & Dummett, M. (2013). The History of the Occult Tarot. Prelude Books.

- Eakins, P. (1992). Tarot of the Spirit. Weiser Books.

- Farley, H. (2009). A Cultural History of Tarot: From Entertainment to Esotericism. IB Tauris Publishers.

- Nichols, S. (1980). Jung and Tarot: An archetypal journey. Weiser Books.

- Pollack, R. (2009). Seventy-eight degrees of wisdom: A book of tarot. Weiser Books.

- Regardie, I., Monnastre, C., & Weschcke, C. L. (1989). The Golden Dawn: a complete course in practical ceremonial magic: the original account of the teachings, rites, and ceremonies of the Hermetic Order of the Golden Dawn (Stella Matutina). Llewellyn Worldwide.

- Sosteric, M. (2014). A sociology of tarot. Canadian Journal of Sociology/Cahiers canadiens de sociologie, 39(3), 357-392.

- Thierens, A. E. (2003). The General Book of the Tarot. Wildside Press LLC.

- Waite, A. E. (1971). The pictorial key to the tarot. Health Research Books.

- Wood, J. (1998). The Celtic tarot and the secret tradition: A study in modern legend making. Folklore, 109(1-2), 15-24.

PODCASTS

- The Astrology Podcast https://theastrologypodcast.com/
- Between the Worlds Podcast https://between-the-worlds-podcast.simplecast.com/
- The Tarot Coven Podcast https://www.tarotcovenpodcast.com/
- Tarot for the Wild Soul https://www.tarotforthewildsoul.com/

ACKNOWLEDGMENTS

This book was created as a collaboration between Queen Raven Tarot and Latte Books to produce a reference book while keeping a seasoned reader anonymous – for now.

We express infinite gratitude to the long line of women readers from Celtic and Indigenous Pacific Islander traditions who have shaped these channeled messages, many of whom were forced to the margins and practiced their gifts in the shadows due to patriarchal religious dogma that has endured for over a thousand years. May others feel safe in connecting with their Higher Self and may you all continue to bring the light, much like the Hermit, in every dark corner that needs your warmth.

Finally, thank you to the Universe for providing this wonderful gift, in addition to spirit guides, ancestors, and all forms of muses that continue to whisper into our ears.

ABOUT LATTE BOOKS

Latte Books is a London-based independent press that thrives on coffee and wanderlust. From artistically designed covers to otherworldly lucid content, we live for diverse perspectives that offer readers a glimpse into worlds and lives they might not otherwise know. Intersectionality in socioeconomic class, culture, gender, race, veteran status, orientation, and/or disability – this is what we crave. We take pride in publishing new and groundbreaking books that are willing to take literary risks and bring us along for the journey. We're committed to making diverse books accessible to readers across the world, showcasing writers who are investing their talents in creating thought-provoking works of art.

Learn more at lattebooks.com

Made in the USA
Las Vegas, NV
09 December 2021

36743808R00187